SUB CITY: YOUNG PEOPLE, HOMELESSNESS AND CRIME

Sub City: Young People, Homelessness and Crime

JULIA WARDHAUGH
University of Wales Bangor

Ashgate

Aldershot • Brookfield USA • Singapore • Sydney

Published by
Ashgate Publishing Ltd
Gower House
Croft Road
Aldershot
Hants GU11 3HR
England

Ashgate Publishing Company
Old Post Road
Brookfield
Vermont 05036
USA

Ashgate website: http://www.ashgate.com

British Library Cataloguing in Publication Data
Wardhaugh, Julia, 1960-
    Sub city : young people, homelessness and crime
    1. Homeless youth 2. Homelessness 3. Crime
    I. Title
    362.7'4

Library of Congress Catalog Card Number: 99-76348

ISBN 1 85972 510 4

Printed in Great Britain by
Antony Rowe Ltd, Chippenham, Wiltshire

Contents

List of Figures

Acknowledgements

Three research projects form the empirical basis of this book. The most extensive was that funded by the Economic and Social Research Council (ESRC) from 1992-95 (reference number R000233540). Thanks are therefore due to the ESRC for supporting the Young People, Lawbreaking, Criminalisation and Homelessness in Three Central England Cities (or the Three Cities Project). The joint grant-holders and co-directors of this project were Julia Wardhaugh (University of Wales Bangor) and Pat Carlen (University of Bath), and the research assistant was Paul Bridges. The qualitative fieldwork was conducted by Julia Wardhaugh and Paul Bridges. My thanks to Paul Bridges for conducting a few of the interviews cited in this work, and for the thoughts and experiences we shared while working together on this project. At the time of the project all the research staff were at the University of Keele.

The analysis of rural homelessness and crime derives from my involvement in two small research projects. The first was conducted in Shropshire in 1992, and was funded by Shropshire probation service, Shrewsbury and Atcham Borough Council, District of the Wrekin Council, Bridgnorth District Council, Council of the Borough of Oswestry, North Shropshire District Council, Stonham Housing Association, Adullam Homes Housing Association and Telford Christian Council. Pat Carlen was the grantholder on this Shropshire Single Homelessness project. The second rural-based project arose from a small grant made to me in 1998 by the University of Wales Bangor for the investigation of homelessness and begging in north Wales: I am grateful to them and to Jane Jones for her work as research assistant on this project.

In the course of these three projects contact was made with numerous agencies and individuals, and they all without exception offered insights from their own experience. My thanks are offered to all those named here. In Birmingham: West Midlands probation service (Homeless Offenders' Unit); Birmingham Standing Committee for Single Homelessness; West Midlands police; Carole Gething House, New Boot, Tennyson House and Trentham House hostels (all St. Basil's); St. Basil's Centre; HARP; Youthlink; Catalyst; Birmingham City Council Housing Department; LINK advice service; St.Martin's drop-in centre. In Manchester: the *Big Issue* offices;

Minshull Street day centre (Greater Manchester probation service); Shades youth advice centre; New Beswick House hostel; Greater Manchester CHAR; Lifeshare; Albert Kennedy Trust; the Survivors' Project; Manchester Housing Consortium (later known as Creative Support); Chorlton bail hostel; Stopover hostel. In North Wales: Sylfaen, a Children's Society youth project; the *Big Issue* offices, Bangor; Conwy County Youth Homlessness Forum. In Shropshire: STAY, Brunel House, Chiltern House and London House hostels; Homeless in Oswestry Action Project; Youth in Crisis, Telford; Shelter Shrewsbury; Shrewsbury Christian centre; South Shropshire Young Persons Housing Project; South Shropshire Housing Association; Wrekin Housing Task Force; Telford Christian Council; Shrewsbury Youth Centre; and staff from each of the agencies funding this project. In Stoke-on-Trent: Potteries Young Homeless Project; Resettlement Project North Staffs; Shelton Neighbourhood Centre; Salvation Army hostel; YMCA hostel; St. Mark's night shelter; Granville House hostel; Potteries Housing Association; Department of Social Security, Hanley and Longton; Stoke-on-Trent City Council Housing Department; North Staffordshire Housing Consortium; North Staffordshire probation service; Staffordshire police; Staffordshire social services; Wenger House probation hostel; Citizens Advice bureau (Longton). In Wolverhampton: Haven housing project. My thanks go also to the senior probation officers at HM Brinsford and HM Hindley Young Offenders' Institutions.

Some of the material included in chapter one appears as '"Down and Outers": fieldwork among street homeless people' in R.D.King and E.Wincup (eds) (forthcoming) *Doing Research in Crime and Justice*, Oxford University Press. Chapter four has appeared as 'The unaccommodated woman: home, homelessness and identity' in *The Sociological Review*, 1999, 47 (1):91-109. An earlier version of the Manchester case-study presented in chapter six was published as 'Homeless in Chinatown: deviance and social control in Cardboard city', in *Sociology*, 1996, 30(4):701-16.

Jane Jones is a graduate student at the University of Wales, Bangor, who is currently conducting some original research in the field of rural criminology. I am very grateful to her for her archival research and contribution of ideas which helped in the writing of the North Wales case-study in chapter two. Particular thanks go to Claire Davis, research administrator at the Centre for Comparative Criminology and Criminal Justice at the University of Wales Bangor, for her skill and patience in preparing the manuscript for publication. I am grateful to Danny, a *Big Issue* vendor in Llandudno, for permission to use his photograph. I would like to thank Her Majesty's Stationery Office for permission to use two extracts from the 1998 Manchester City Centre map, used in chapter six. Thank you to Stephen Carter for permission to use the photograph taken of him while visiting North Wales.

My special thanks go to all the homeless young people who trusted me with their stories: in talking to them I was able to begin to understand some of the meanings of home and homelessness. All personal names used have been changed.

Chronology of the criminalisation of homelessness

1274	First statute restricting almsgiving by monasteries
c.1300	Pauline Christianity replaces Franciscan notion of 'holy poverty'
1349	Penalties introduced for 'idle and valiant' beggars
1351	Restrictions introduced on travelling in search of work
1360-1495	Increasing severity of punishments for vagrancy
1503	Reduction in the levels of some punishments for vagrancy, alongside a shift towards the criminalisation of begging and itineracy
1530	First statute defining beggars as criminals and/or as fakes; increasing severity of punishments, including mutilation of vagrants; development of categories of unlawful behaviour and deviance
1535	Vagrancy punishable by the death penalty for the first time; repeated vagrants defined as felons, enemies of the state
1547	Introduction of branding and enslavement as commonplace punishments for vagrancy; expansion of the category 'vagabond'
1563	Procedures for the badging of beggars formalised
1570-1600	Vagabondage increasingly associated with disorder and crime; new categories of people constructed as a problem, for example young people; increasing use of severe and permanent punishments, such as enslavement and banishment; use of bridewells from 1576 designed in principle, though

rarely in practice, to reform as well as punish vagrants

1662	The Law of Settlement and Removal is passed, sending the poor back to their places of origin: this law was to last for two centuries. Otherwise, the legislation remained largely unchanged from the late-16th to the mid-18th centuries
1743 onwards	Continued expansion and clarification of categories of vagabondage; however little change occurs to the spirit of the legislation, that is, the criminalisation of marginal groups such as beggars and vagrants
1792	Whipping of female vagrants is abolished
1824	Major vagrancy act is passed, rationalising the criminal law and replacing 27 previous vagrancy acts. Three categories of vagrant were retained, and the level of punishments was reduced; this was a 'catch-all' piece of legislation, directed at prostitution and other street offences as well as vagrancy; it has been interpreted as an early example of a 'sus' law; the emphasis was on the punishment rather than reform of vagrants
1832	Peak level of imprisonments for vagrancy
1834	Passage of the New Poor Law
1910-14	High number of prosecutions under 1824 Act
1920-29	Number of prosecutions low and falling; start of massive housebuilding programme (continuing, with lower standards, into the 1930s) to accommodate homeless war veterans, under the slogan 'Homes Fit for Heroes'; many homeless households squat in disused Ministry of Defence buildings
1930s	Sharp decrease in convictions for vagrancy
1935	Vagrancy Act partially decriminalised those sleeping rough; introduction of clauses qualifying the definition of someone as a 'rogue and vagabond' under the 1824 Act: one such condition was that the person was causing, or was likely to cause, a threat to public health
late 1930s	Over 3,500 begging prosecutions per annum
early postwar years	700-900 begging prosecutions per annum

1948	Passage of National Assistance Act, ending the Poor Law and heralding the advent of the Welfare State; homelessness begins to be defined as a welfare rather than law and order problem; local authorities are required to provide temporary accommodation for certain categories of the homeless population
1960s	(Re)discovery of homelessness as a social problem, with especial focus on families and vulnerable youth; establishment of charitable and pressure groups concerned with homelessness
1968	Under 500 prosecutions for begging
1970s	900-1,300 prosecutions for begging per annum
1971	Brennan Committee investigates the implementation of the 1824 Vagrancy Act and concludes that sleeping rough (and to a lesser extent begging) are evidence of social need rather than criminality; prosecutions for sleeping rough at a low level at this time
1974	Report on Vagrancy and Street Offences: once more, vagrancy is linked with other street offences such as prostitution
1977	Housing (Homeless Persons) Act: an important piece of civil rather than criminal legislation dealing with homelessness. This Act introduced a limited concept of 'rights' in terms of access to housing, but retained the old distinction between the deserving and undeserving poor (the unintentionally and intentionally homeless); the local connection amendment to the Act resurrected the Old Poor Law's concern with keeping paupers in their places of origin; the transfer of responsibility for homelessness from social services to housing departments helped to redefine homelessness as a housing rather than social welfare problem
early 1980s	Changes in the welfare system led to a rapid increase in homelessness, especially among the 'new homeless' such as young people; there was some increase in public sympathy for the street homeless and visibly destitute
late 1980s	Prosecutions for begging and sleeping rough increase rapidly, as limited sympathy evaporates and as the 'new homeless' rapidly become criminalised; the interpretation of the 1977 Act becomes progressively narrowed, and the use of short-term responses increases

late 1980s - early 1990s	Charitable and pressure groups attempt to introduce a number of legal developments, such as the badging (and therefore legitimation) of *Big Issue* vendors; the establishment of voting rights for rough sleepers in cities such as Manchester; and the (unsuccessful) End the Vagrancy Act campaigns
1991	Rough sleepers are included in the national census for the first time
1994	Criminal Justice and Public Order Act criminalises the formerly civil offences of travelling and squatting
1996	Housing Act reduces the availability of emergency accommodation and expands the scope of the Rough Sleepers' Initiative

Prologue

This chapter presents the lives of six homeless people as told in their own words. These can not be described as typical stories as each person is an individual and their lives are unique. Nevertheless, as their stories are complex they inevitably resonate with at least some aspects of other lives in other places. Much of the diversity among homeless people can be found here: women and men; black, white and Asian people; victims and offenders; single people and parents; country-dwellers and city people; squatters, travellers, hostel-dwellers and rough sleepers.

These narratives have been chosen to open this book because they allow homeless people to emerge from the shadows and to take centre-stage for a time. Each of their stories prefigures some of the major themes developed in later chapters, for example the gendered experience of home and homelessness in chapter four, victimisation of the homeless in chapter five, and the regulation of homeless spaces and places in chapter six.

These six people - Dill, Ellie, Katy, Kaz, Michael and Shanaz - tell their own tales but the author is there off-stage listening to them and asking questions, and later selecting and editing their life stories. While much is told here much else is left out, for these are simply fragments of homeless lives, selected aspects of a much larger and more complex picture. They serve nonetheless to lead us directly into the subject matter of this book: young people, homelessness and crime.

Dill - 'I was homeless from the time I was thirteen'

Dill was a white man aged twenty years. Born in Manchester and homeless since the age of thirteen, he had travelled extensively through Wales and England, adopting an itinerant lifestyle. The Big Issue - the success story for homeless people of the 1980s and 1990s - had allowed him to make a living of sorts and to hold some hopes for the future. Dill told his story sitting outside Cathedral Gardens in Bangor, while local police were trying to move on some of his homeless friends.

I was born in Manchester and lived there till I was thirteen when I left care. Then went down south and into a hostel till I got chucked out of there at about fourteen. I was homeless down there. How it happened, to cut a long story short, when I was little my dad was nasty to me, a real bastard. That's why I was in care, he used to abuse me and that. When I was sixteen I was still homeless, I was homeless from the time I was thirteen, and I wanted to see me dad, I wanted a father so I got in touch with him when he come out of prison. I stayed with him for a couple of weeks and then it turned nasty, he told all his mates about what happened when I was a kid, he turned everyone against me. So I left [and went] down south again, homeless again, got in fights and everything.

Then I got in with the marquees down Gloucester way, travelling round for a couple of years just putting up marquees, that was buzzing that was. Then I left, became homeless again. So I went to Manchester to see my mum, I was there till about four months ago. I was homeless there and got into a few fights, there was loads of people wanted to kick me head [in] 'cause they thought I was someone else. So I left Manchester and came to Bangor with me bird. I don't like the cities 'cause I get a load of shit, 'specially being on the streets. It's quieter here, you've got homeless people in the town, but you haven't got any badheads. Not like in Piccadilly ... I was getting loads of hassle when I was in Manchester and so I thought 'Bangor, a small town, somewhere quiet by the sea'. It's all right here, I try to keep myself to myself 'cause that's what I'm used to. I like to work an area out, and when I have worked it out I like to move again, else I get bored with it.

When I first came here I was homeless, I slept on the island [Anglesey] at first for a couple of days before I came into Bangor and said 'look, anything for me?', and they said there's not much but go along to the *Big Issue* and they'll get you badged up, give you a bowl of soup, although they don't do that no more. It's all right selling the *Big Issue*, you could class it as a job, although other people don't. A bloke told me I was spending all my effing money on beer, and I thought 'why not? I do a job'. Just 'cause I'm selling the *Issue* doesn't mean I can't do the things other people do with their money. I sell the *Issue* every day, I have to. There's two best pitches in town, there's [WH] Smith's and there's Thresher's, and I've got Thresher's. It's a good spot, 'cause you've got all the people coming down the High Street from the train station, and I'm also catching people from the lower town.

If I make twenty pounds before 12 or 2 o'clock I'll finish then. I set an average of what I need for the day, for food, what I drink, or if I've got a fine to pay. Twenty, thirty pounds a day. Sometimes I can only make a fiver, which is even worse, 'cause I've not got enough for the next day's *Issues*, so that means I'm only going to make a fiver the next day, whereas if I make twenty pound one day I can use ten pound for food and whatever, and ten pound to buy twenty *Issues* next morning. It depends - selling - different days and different people. The tourists usually buy them, and I've got my regular customers as well. When I'm not selling I go to the pub, get pissed up, or try not to get pissed up 'cause I'm trying to dry up from alcohol

2

at the moment. Just hang about round the cathedral or down by the benches. Once I'm in a place I don't tend to move about much, just stay in that place.

There's a couple of bad things happened since I've been homeless. When I was fourteen I was in Blackpool selling lighters, and walked into a night-club and there was all these people saying 'what's your story?' and I said 'I'm homeless, I'm just trying to sell some lighters', and they dragged me outside and gave me a kicking, do you know what I mean? I battered a few of them, but I got the worst of it. They just did it 'cause I was homeless. Then when I was down south in Gloucester someone gave me some nice trainers, and some guy pulled out a knife when I was asleep, pissed up, and I woke up with the trainers gone and a big gash on me. I was looking for him next day to beat his face in, to get him back for that, but he got away.

I've been done by the police, I've been woke up by them, torch shone in my face, saying 'sorry mate, you can't sleep here'. Different places, that was, Southampton, Plymouth, Cheltenham, all over down there. They just move you on, but I have been charged for begging, and they just gave me a conditional discharge. After that I wasn't allowed in that town again, it was somewhere in the Forest of Dean. It's OK around here, as I'm getting to know more people, it's all right. But I'm scared that, 'cause I've had bad experiences, that there's rumours going around about me and I'll get into fights. So I just keep myself to myself. People just get bored and think 'oh, we'll take the piss out of him for the day'. It's better here than in the cities, 'cause like Piccadilly [Manchester] can be tough.

Ellie - 'With my dog for company'

Ellie was in many ways indistinguishable from other young people in the student cathedral city of Bangor - aged eighteen and from a middle-class background, she had adopted the traveller clothes and lifestyle popular with many of her contemporaries. However, Ellie had experienced a dislocated family background and was now homeless.

Originally I come from Portsmouth, although I consider Shropshire my second home. I used to live in Portsmouth with my dad, it's a very long story but basically he treated me badly and we didn't get on. And because of his position in society - you can tell from my voice that I'm pretty posh - he bent things round and they became my fault. So I moved away to live with my mum, in Bridgnorth in Shropshire. It didn't work for me, it wasn't my home, I didn't get on with my step-dad that well. I just up and left one day. I was with Nik in Shrewsbury, that's where I went first when I left, and we just decided to go travelling together. We travelled all over in Wales and then came to Bangor, and we've both stayed here ever since, even though we've split up now. I've gone out travelling a few times, but I've made this place my base, 'cause everyone's really friendly here.

The police, they're not too sure about the rules round here. For example, there's Brewery Fields, you know that protest site? I was there for about a week or so, I was doing lock-ons, which is where you put your arm down this drainpipe that's been concreted into the ground. On the eviction day,

3

which was my day off luckily, the police came along and they barricaded themselves around everyone, and they did torture them, they got these clamps and attached them to people's wrists and pulled them tighter and tighter, seriously bruising bones. That's just a simple example of the tone they take towards people like us around here. They just can't be bothered being polite.

Around Bangor, if you get moved on, I mean I was arrested for begging the day that my dog died. They sometimes get sneaky and get undercover cops walking past, and then if you beg them they can arrest you, little tricks like that. That happened to me, I got taken to Caernarfon police station. The thing is I'm lucky, you see, because unlike lots of people around here I've figured it all out in the sense of I'm very good at blagging, 'cause I've got a posh accent. I think part of the problem of the police is partly caused by us as well, like all the travellers round here walk about trying to be all cool and hard and that. They want to put across that they're not to be messed with, and so when the police do have to mess with them they mess with them more, because of the image. But they feel they have to put that image [across] so no-one will mess with them when they're sleeping on the street, or when they're in a different place.

But for me what's worked best is being polite. When I got arrested and taken to Caernarfon, all I got was an informal warning, and they even gave me a lift back to Bangor (laughs). I was making friends with them, you've just got to pretend to be polite. I've been arrested quite a few times. I've been arrested for being drunk and disorderly a number of times, and that's the time when they do get pretty hefty, 'cause they think you're just another pisshead and you're not going to remember in the morning.

I used to sell the *Big Issue* but I've decided I prefer busking, playing the penny whistle. I can make £35 or £40 in a day. Is it better in the summer? I've mixed views on that, in the winter, when people walk past they look at you and they feel the cold. So subconsciously they think 'that person's sleeping out tonight, and I'd hate to be sitting down there in the cold, asking people for money'. In the summer it depends the mood of the day, if it's sunny like today you get people all happy and chucking money at you, so the summer's better because you're in a better mood yourself.

It depends on the place, 'cause some towns are morning towns and some towns are afternoon towns. That's what I've found, that in different towns people get up at different times and do things at different times, it's like routines. Generally Bangor is an afternoon town. For *Big Issue* selling Monday is the best day, because it comes out on a Monday. With busking I find Wednesdays are quite good, I can't think of the psychology behind it. I don't like busking on Saturdays 'cause it's so hectic and there's so many people. I like to be one of those people that's chilled out, playing background music for people to stumble across as they're walking past.

I come into Bangor most of the time, but I go all over the place. Holyhead's a good place, no-one's discovered it yet, but I can make about twenty-two quid in about two hours, three hours there. You can do Caernarfon, but everyone's very Welsh in Caernarfon, so it's a bit dodgy if you're English and playing Irish tunes, 'cause you might get someone coming along and beating you up. There's a lot of lads round there, if you

4

know what I mean. I've done Llandudno, but it's not that good, this was ages ago. Rhyl's OK, it's another average Bangor-type town, you make the same sort of money. If you're busking all day you can make about twenty-five quid, and that's enough to see me through for a few days.

I like making music for people. And there's another point about begging, busking, everyone has a go at us for doing that, taking money off people. The point is if people don't want to give us their money, then they won't give us their money. 'Cause human beings are like that, it's in our instincts, if we don't want to give something to someone then we won't. If we're not too bothered then we might be blagged into it. That's why I like busking because I'm not saying anything to anyone, I'm just playing my music. So if someone did come and have a go at me and say 'oh, you effing beggars', I don't know whether you want swear words in, I can just say 'I'm not begging, I'm just playing my music to you, you don't have to drop me any money, I'm getting pleasure out of it myself'. When I was selling the *Big Issue* I had people coming up to me and saying 'you're not homeless', and I'm like 'are you judging me?' And it's just because I'm looking clean or whatever, although I'm not looking clean at the moment. With busking I can just sit down and chill out, although it gets quite tiring.

I'm staying with a friend in Anglesey at the moment, although I'm going travelling pretty soon. Then I'll come back here, because as I said I like to make Bangor my base. Most of the time I'm travelling. I come back here and I spend maybe a few weeks here, and go back out again. Basically I make myself a destination, and then I just go in that direction, and stop in towns along the way. Sometimes I stop in a town for a week, depends if I make any friends or not. I just hitch on my own, with my dog for company. He's the best.

Katy - 'I've been institutionalised for so long'

Katy was a 23-year old white Birmingham woman who was living in a hostel for homeless women and their babies. Physically abused by her mother and sexually abused by her step-father, Katy described herself as never having known a family and home. Her homeless years have been spent in a struggle with alcoholism, and in a search for home and security.

How I came to be homeless? Well, I decided to get out when I was sixteen. Me mum, every time she was drunk, she just had a temper and stuff. And her boyfriend, she was with him since I was two. I never liked him anyway. Me mum used to say that every time he looked at me I'd always cry. At first, 'cause I was drinking at the time, I just went to different lads' houses, and friends' houses. This was in Oldham. Then I went in to sort the drink problem out. Then I went to a clinic and then I came here. It was alcohol mostly, and some gas and a few sleeping tablets here and there. But I'd always drink alone though. I'd always drink alone.

I went into one hostel but I was still drinking then. And then they give me an ultimatum to cut down the drink, or to leave. So I left and went into another

5

rehab [rehabilitation unit]. That was horrible, 'cause I was the only woman there, the rest of them was men, and I felt really uncomfortable, but I was only there for about four months. I think when I left there, I set myself up to drink 'cause I went back to the drink anyway, but I wasn't drinking as much.

It's really nice here, you get a lot of support from the staff, and a lot of residents as well. There's a lot of bitchiness though, so I just like keep myself to myself, I just go out. It's quiet though, I mean even though there's babies around, it's quiet. People don't really mix here, after eleven o' clock they lock the doors, so we can't go out and go and chat to the other girls. So it's quite boring sometimes. They get you a flat at the end of twelve months. But I don't really want a flat, I want shared or sheltered [accommodation], 'cause I'm used to being like around a lot of people, so I'd prefer that. I wouldn't like my own flat, 'cause even though I've got the baby I'd still be scared to be on my own.

No I didn't really tell anybody [about the child abuse she experienced]. No, I couldn't, I couldn't go out. No, I couldn't see boyfriends or see my mates. And when I did go out I'd just stay on the front of the house. No, he'd want me all to himself. Well, it was mostly the drink what caused the problem really. I mean I suppose homelessness, well drinking was connected to it. Yeah, it was because places where I used to go, friends or anything, they didn't really like me drinking. I'd only stop a couple of nights, but I knew that they wanted me out anyway.

One of the worst things about being homeless is at Christmas seeing families through the window enjoying themselves and thinking 'I'm out in the cold'. The hostel is an institution, and all the hostels I've been in are institutions, and that's why I don't want my own flat, because I've been institutionalised for so long, three years, and always depended on people really. I feel safe in a hostel, but there again even though there's people around, you still feel alone.

I don't really think you can predict the future, but I would like a nice steady job, my own flat, and not being scared to stay at home, and being a career woman I think, that's what I would want. When I say to people 'Oh, I'm in a hostel', they just look at me funny, as though to say 'why?' Or if they're living at home, then they'll brag about what it's like to live at home with parents of their own. It makes me feel that I'm lower than them, like they're higher than me, and they're belittling me. And because they've got a home, then they're different to what I am.

Did I ever get into trouble? I used to have fights when I was drunk. 'Cause when you're drunk you don't bother, you just go up to people and say anything, and I used to really piss people off as well. 'Cause the local what I used to go in, I'd have a drink before I go in obviously to get the confidence to talk to people. And I'd always go up to fellows asking them for a drink and that, and the dirty evil looks what I used to get off the regulars who used to go in there.

I've been picked up twice by the police. Once for drinking on a main road, and being unconscious and that. And they picked me up once 'cause I ran away from home. They picked me up about five hours later and took me back. But I was saying to them 'no, I'm too scared to go back, I don't want to go back'. And when I got back home, they [the police] says 'Will anything happen to her?' And obviously, they [her mother and stepfather] said no. But he did anyway. Once I did tell someone that I was getting hit, and I phoned a social worker up, and the NSPCC. One person came out and they couldn't do anything 'cause I didn't have any bruises. I was about thirteen or fourteen then. I just felt disbelieved by everyone. And I couldn't run anywhere, and I was trapped and everything. But I suppose I could have classed myself homeless then 'cause it wasn't really a home. Yeah, because a home, it's a family, a good family atmosphere, and you do things together. The only time I'd had a family atmosphere is when I was fostered and that was about it. When I was sixteen I escaped.

I think the world's getting worse now [rather] than better ... the IRA will be over here soon. It gets me really paranoid sometimes to go out. Just in case there's a man with a shotgun or something. 'Cause there was a bomb scare when I was in Corporation Street, I think it was a long time ago. So I wouldn't go up for a couple of weeks. If I'm walking down the street I think there's somebody following me or something, and I get really paranoid. Sometimes it stops me going out, I ask other people to go to the shops with me, 'cause I get really scared.

Kaz - 'The worst thing about being homeless is the winter really'

Kaz was a young white man of 23 years who had been homeless since the age of sixteen. His homeless career had taken him to various places in the south and north of England, where he spent his time squatting or sleeping rough. His income came from activities such as begging and selling the Big Issue.

I was thrown out when I was sixteen, then slept on a friend's floor and then couldn't stay there any longer so then [I] went on the streets, found myself a squat. Squatted with a few people, shared a house with them, then we got evicted so broke into another squat, so on and so on and so on, moved to a few different ones. Then I moved down south with a friend, living in the back of a truck, just went round a bit like, ended up living in a coach, then ended up in a car with me mate (laughter). [We were] dossing around, lived in Bristol and London, Hampshire, Basingstoke, down Cornwall ... Truro, down Cornwall. Come back up here in '89. Found another squat, just dossing around in a few different squats like till about 1990, then got evicted and I was back on the street again.

I'm sleeping right down the bottom of Deansgate where all the canals meet. On the canal basin, there's loads of arches under there, we sleep down there. It's quiet there, but there's loads of police round there as well. You're pretty safe round there except for when they're waking you up make sure you're not dead (laughs). There's nobody round there at night-time, but you meet a few weirdos down there (laughs). Just nutters you know, just people what are out and about all night, just daft.

They don't bother you, just there's that many places down there anyway, usually [you do] get hassled when they're down there, [but not if] you know what you're doing. It's obvious what I'm doing because I'm sleeping on the floor. But the coppers are all right with me, they're entitled to move me on. [There's] no hassle off them. [I] usually do [my] sitting in the town, but there again you've [those people who are] out and about who don't want to see that

7

sort of stuff do they? They like to think that there's no homeless people in Manchester.

They [the police] wanna nick you all the time and things like that. The thing what I'm up for bail for now, I was in town, [we] was all drinking in town, which we do every day like, but not at the moment. And they set the dogs on us all and [they're] coming out with injunctions and what have you. So we walked off away from them, but they just kept following us across the [Piccadilly] Gardens, and they started letting the dogs off and hitting people that were out and about with truncheons and everything, so we just ended up fighting with them, know what I mean. [They] provoked us too much. So I'm pleading not guilty 'cause I can't remember what I did 'cause I was drunk (laughs).

As for begging [if] you haven't got enough for something to eat and they move you on, I'll have to go back until I have got enough for something to eat. So when they see you again they nick you. [I've] been sat in the Square, I was there one day, I was just sat on a bench drinking a cup of tea and he [a police officer] come up and said 'I just seen you begging', and I says 'I'm trying to drink a cup of tea'. He says 'well as far as I'm concerned I've seen you with your hand out begging, so I want you to go'. You know, it's your word against theirs, know what I mean? If they're in a bad mood you just keep out of their way.

I went to court once, fifty pound I got fined for begging. I've had a sixty pound fine for begging as well. I don't know how you're expected to pay for it. [I] couldn't afford it anyway, I didn't pay it. I don't know why they do it 'cause it costs them more than fifty pounds to arrest you, to put you through all the arrest procedure, taking you in and feeding you. And if you get nicked on a Friday, they leave you in till Monday. All the money they go through keeping you and feeding you, it costs them more than fifty quid just to give you a fine for fifty quid. Don't see the point.

I think at the moment [August 1994] with the Criminal Justice Bill they wanna get through, they gotta prove that crimes are up like. So they go round and they hassle people, and they nick loads of people. I think that's what that Saturday was all about. And the more arrests and serious charges the better, they've got more chance of getting it through.

The worst thing about being homeless is the winter really. You wake up in the morning and everything's damp and what have you. Bronchitis sets off as well, late at night when it's starting to get cool and get damp, the air's damp and especially in the morning you just cough, coughing all the time and being sick and everything. Makes you sick. There's a GP down on Canal Street or somewhere like that, there's a GP what does homeless people, if you drop in down there. There's a day when you can go in and see a doctor. Like the last time I seen a doctor I got diagnosed with bronchitis, that was quite a long time ago.

And you get sore feet (laughs). You know, at the moment I've got a decent pair of boots, but if you have a pair that's split and everything, you end up with trench foot. 'Cause you're in wet boots all the time. You can take them off, but you've got more chance of them drying on your feet. If you take them off and they go hard, and they're uncomfortable to walk in.

The other problem is eating, it's like if you get somewhere quiet enough, like waste ground or what have you, you can usually buy some dinner, find odd bricks and build a little thing. Find an old cooker, rip the grill tray out, put that over it and usually light the fire and cook things like that. But otherwise it's like you just got to eat out all the time, it's expensive. People don't realise how expensive it is, paying a fiver for a meal. If you don't know where to go for it. But I used to go to day centres and like the cathedral [you can] get one for about a quid. But it's the walk isn't it, you got to walk there.

How do I spend my days? I'll sell the *Issue* and then I'd have a drink ... then I'd ...(long pause) ... phew ... nothing, don't know like, find a few mates and sit around. Sometimes if there's no one around, go in library and get something, library's all right. Just sit round like, depends if it's sunny. When it's cold it's just go in a cafe and spend as much as you can on cups of tea and make them last you.

The city centre is pretty crap, know what I mean, I used to go sit down Salford cathedral. You get bored with the people who're there, some of the people, you get the odd one or two who sit there mithering you and all that. You can't cope with it. I go and find a nice quiet café and sit and drink cups of tea, coffee, what have you. A bit of peace and quiet. Better than being in the town centre all the time, you don't realise how much it's all rush, rush.

London's worse, got more chance of getting a kicking down there as well. Don't like it, don't like London one little bit, it's a horrible place. There was a few people on this church ground. So we had a laugh, didn't go begging or nothing while I was there, we all got giros when we was down there, so we just made them last. Bought a load of food in, lit fires and everything to cook on so ... Other than that you could always scrounge something from somewhere, skips for old food that was thrown out from supermarkets. It's all right, no need to beg down there. Used to beg in Basingstoke, then it got pretty heavy down there 'cause the security guards used to move you out there all the time, 'cause they was doing something with the city centre. So we moved out.

I'm selling papers [*Big Issue*] at the moment. I used to sell them in the precinct, but then they moved me out the precinct so I sell them on Sun Street. Just as good like but not, you don't sell them as fast. Used to sell them really fast when I was sat in the precinct. No, they're trying recreate the city centre aren't they? Don't help them much me hanging round selling the *Issues*. I can't see what problem it makes though. I could be a *Manchester Evening News* vendor couldn't I? It's all right for buskers, you know it probably makes the place look dainty or something, having buskers round, something for the tourists to look at.

I'm not supposed to be in town, I only come as far as here, get paid and get a bus back to Stockport. 'Cause like I'm barred from the city centre. I've got a ban. Still go out to clubs like (laughs), just have to be careful. Well it's something to do ain't it, rather than getting your head down dead early. When I was down London there was some clubs down there they're a fiver to get in, all right, but you'd pay a fiver for bed and breakfast, and they go from like nine o'clock till about seven in the morning. It's like exciting in there while you're in there, rather than paying a fiver for bed and breakfast. You can fall asleep in a club anyway, so it never used to bother you.

I know a lot of people in Manchester, I can't walk through Manchester without going 'all right, how you doing', and even through Stockport since I've been there you just get to know people really quickly. Like I know all the policemen up there now anyway. Not 'cause I've done owt wrong since I've been there, I just like to talk to them. The male coppers don't talk much, know what I mean, they just walk past, they're all big lads in Stockport the coppers. But the women coppers they'll stop and talk to you, they're really friendly and everything. I've had no hassle, not from the police. I have off the security guards, move me here and there and whatever, but the police have never bothered.

Begging's the worst thing, you get loads of abuse for doing that. When I used to beg I used to get spat at and kicked at and everything. But after a bit you learn to take it 'cause if not you get in for a fight every five minutes, so you just sit there, you've got to learn to ignore it. It depends on how bad it is, you get the ones that when they come out the pubs, there's a gang of them. They all crowd round you and you're sat on the floor ... so you just got to sit there and just ignore it. They get bored after a bit if you don't do owt and they just walk off.

I had a guy try and stab me once, when I asked him for fifty pence. Just pulled a knife, he was just with his mates. Begging on Friday nights and Saturday nights is out of the question. So you just do it in the day. It's funny, women usually get hassled for sex and we just get kicked in (laughter).

Michael - 'I'll always be on my own'

Michael was a twenty-five year-old man of Jamaican and white British parentage. After a childhood spent in care, he spent his adult years wandering from place to place in the north of England. Someone who preferred to be on his own, Michael was one of those street people who came into little contact with agencies on the homelessness circuit. Although he had spent many homeless years in Manchester, he had not known of the existence of the drop-in centre where our conversation took place.

Well the way I became homeless was when I lost me job, I was working in Dewsbury in West Yorkshire. That's where the home was, when I went sixteen that's when I left it. I went to me friend's flat, stopped there for about a few months. Got a couple of jobs, well I got one job, got fired. Every job I've had I've got fired from, it's me own fault really just not getting up in the morning. After I got sacked I started moving around, went to Leeds and stopped in Leeds for a bit. Stopped in a bloody DHSS hostel, didn't really like it 'cause a lot of the guys who was in there was on drugs. No I never got into drugs. I've always hated needles since I was a kid. And they had smack in silver foil and stuff like that. I don't know why it just never appealed to me. I did get into sniffing gas at one point.

It's pointless me going in a bed and breakfast because if I did that I wouldn't be able to do what I can do, I can travel all over the place. I was getting my money and moving from Manchester, moving all over the place. Sometimes I go to Liverpool, wherever I know a few people I'll go there. I don't get in touch with any agencies at all. I got on housing lists in loads of places. I stopped in a lot of cities in the country, I been to London once. I went down and I found out it's the worst place to go.

But there's not a lot of black guys on the streets you know. With me it's a lot different 'cause some people say 'well what are you doing on the streets', because if you're a black guy you're supposed to know every other black guy that comes along. Well it's not like that. Like I went up north of the country and there's not a lot of black guys up north. I've been as far as Newcastle. The first time I went there I knew nobody up there, I thought I'll go up there 'cause it's the furthest away I could get. When I was in the city centre I was getting called all kinds of stuff, always you black bastard, 'cause there's no blacks around. There's a few Asians in Newcastle you know, but no black people.

Well, I thought I've never been able to beg, I've never been like that you know, 'cause it's always embarrassing. So that's something I've never done, I've never begged for money, I've always tried to keep myself clean. Sometimes when I've got a bit down you'll get some people coming up to you and saying 'what you doing on the streets man?' You see some black guys going out on the town saying 'you shouldn't be on the street, what you doing on the streets, you're showing yourself up'. [But] it's just the same for everybody you know, thousands of people all over are on the streets, know what I mean. It's a loss of pride, 'cause people think, when it comes to white people they just presume that all the black people know each other.

If I was in Bradford and you was Indian or you was Pakistani and you was on the street, I don't think you'd be on the streets for long. 'Cause it's sort of one big community. Like you see people begging on the streets but you never see Asians begging on the streets. I think if they was seen to do that, even if one of their relatives seen them doing that, they would be disgraced. [But] like in India or Pakistan the people are doing that naturally on the streets. So I don't know why they see it as so disgraceful over here. I'm not Asian, 'cause a lot of people mistake me for that, like if I was in Bradford a lot of people come up to me and speak in Pakistani and I don't know the first word, but they take me for Asian.

Have I been a victim of crime? Oh well you've just got to sort of turn a blind eye you know. I haven't been a victim of crime myself. I've been asked for money sometimes when I've been paid and they think I've got money, they'll ask me for money and I'll just say 'no I haven't got nothing'. It's different because I've been assaulted a few times as well. That's mainly because of my colour it's not because I'm homeless. It's all different cities and that, and I find that the further north you go the worse it is. Further north, I'm talking north from Leeds, the worse it is. I've been called black bastard and stuff. It probably gets easier as you go south, Birmingham or if you go down London. If you lived in somewhere like Notting Hill or Brixton, see there's none of it down there, it's just as you get north of the country I find. That's where I've had most trouble.

Yes I've had threats, when I've walked into some pubs sometimes I've got dirty looks. If I walk into a pub and there's no black people in the pub, then I know straight away I shouldn't be in there, so I drink up and go off. They don't have to say anything, it's just the attitude. Even the bar staff, it's just the attitude. You know straight away that's a hint to leave the pub. 'Cause by law they can't say 'oh you can't come in here because you're black', it's against the law you see. But they hint to make you go.

I've never been insulted racially by the homeless, never in my life. I've never heard of one incident of racial abuse, you know like in Piccadilly Gardens there's about sixty people sometimes at night, there's not once I've ever heard that. That's the only time I've never heard it with so many people as well. Even if there's an Indian guy come up he never gets called nothing. It's the only place

I've never heard it on the streets. It's funny that, you expect it to be mostly on the streets as well. No matter what colour you are they look after you, they always respect one another.

The worst thing about being on the streets is not having anywhere to bloody get a wash in the morning, or get a shave. Unless I know somebody who's got a flat and I can call in and have a wash and a shave. The worst thing about it is walking around the street the next day filthy, you feel disgusting. People are going to work in the morning and they're looking at you, giving you a funny look. You feel filthy, that's the worst thing for me.

If you've got something of value you'll get it robbed, there's no doubt about that, you'll get it robbed. The first person who's got any chance of getting hold of it they'll take it straight away. Can't trust nobody, that's one thing you can't do, you can't trust them on the streets you see. No matter how good a friend they might seem, you never get too close, you see I never get too close to anybody. 'Cause if you start getting too close to somebody that's when I think they start taking advantage of you. You talk to them and be friends with them and all that kind of thing, but you don't get too close. That's how I've found it anyway because I've always been on my own. Since I've been a kid and that's the way I'll stay. I'll always be on my own.

Well, my time is always spent in the libraries. No matter where I am, say if I'm here [Manchester] or in Huddersfield or Leeds. You can go in libraries any time of the day, and if it's not a museum it's a library, anywhere where it's free. As long as it's not setting me back any money and it's a decent environment, say there's nobody boozing and all that. I'll read anything as long as it's killing time. You see the trouble with me is I'm just waiting from one pay-day to the next, that's all. That's why the years just go, your years just fly by. You wait every two weeks and you only get paid twice a month. The years just fly by, for me they do anyway. In the last six years I haven't done nothing but wait for one pay day to the next. I expect to do that for the rest of my life, unless I go home. There's just no jobs.

I was telling somebody, another guy like me but he's full Jamaican, he's not on the streets exactly he's in a bed and breakfast, and he was telling me that he couldn't get a job because of his colour. I says that in a few years time you'll have to leave the country. I see that all blacks will have to leave Britain in the next ten years, any black person with sense will leave Europe. If they don't leave on their own they'll be forced out anyway, that's what I think's coming. I mean it happened in the thirties, it happened in the thirties but it was the Jews who caught it in the thirties. It's anybody now, if you're black or you're Asian or whatever, you're going to have to leave Europe in the next ten to fifteen years.

No I never think about the future me, it doesn't bother me. In five year's time I'll still be doing what I'm doing now. Depends on how the situation changes 'cause I'll never get the money to leave the country. I'll never have the money to do that. Unless we get a fascist party in government here, we'll be repatriated anyway, that's what I think. Whether we like it or not. They'll give us a couple of thousand pound and send us all off to Africa. They can give me a couple of thousand pound and I'll go to Africa but I won't stay there, I'll bugger off to somewhere else. South-east Asia, where the money's worth a lot more. Maybe in a year's time I might meet a girl and I'll settle down, you never know. Or I could be doing the same but I'll never end up a drunken alcoholic on the streets, I mean that's one thing I don't want to do.

I don't beg at all because it don't get you anywhere. The only people who beg really are if they're on drugs or on alcohol, if they're addicted to something they beg. They've got to do it. 'Cause all the people you see begging on the street they get money anyway, everybody gets social security in this country. I mean there's nobody that can say he doesn't get any money, by law he's got to get it so he must get it. Whatever he does with it, or what she does with it, once they've spent that they've got to beg for more 'cause they need more for what they're addicted to. That's how I see it anyway.

Shanaz - 'Who knows what's going on inside the house? Only me'

Shanaz was a thirty year-old British Asian woman currently living in a hostel for women in Wolverhampton. Originally from Preston she had lost her children to the custody of their father, whom she had left after thirteen years of a violent marriage. Shanaz told her story while sitting in the lounge of the hostel, through tears and with the help of some cigarettes.

Well when I was about seven or eight, me father like, he had a mental problem and he used always want to get the chopper and chop us up. And me mum, to protect us, she used to send us out of the house. We had a grandmother that used to live nearby but she didn't want to know, so we used to have to stay in the alley-way until we see the ambulance come and take him away to hospital. So my mum decided to take him to India to get well, because in India there is a lot of holy healers. So I was left with four brothers, three sisters we were. I was left bringing them up. That was going to school, doing the cooking, them days it was making the coal fire, things like that, cleaning the house. I think me mum must have been away for about a year and then me father died in India.

Me mum didn't know anything about social money nor nothing like that, we lived off family allowance. Some days we used to get a dinner, and some days we didn't. And we used to just sleep on it, go to bed or whatever. Life went on. Me brother left home. Then it was me. Then I got engaged when I was about fourteen, an arranged marriage it was. And I told my mum I didn't want to get married yet, because I never had a bit of space in my life. I get married and first, you know with us not having a boyfriend or anything, you fall in love. He said he were never going to hit me or anything like that. I believed in everything what he said, what he told me.

Then just turned seventeen, just after a month of marriage, got pregnant. Got married in a family where there were seven sisters and three brothers, a father that's disabled and a mother-in-law that used always stay in bed. And I was up from 7 in the morning till 2 in the morning, you know, working for all them, while they used to just get a video and sit down and watch it. But I wasn't allowed go to bed until all of them have had their dinner. Right?

Then after two or three years of living with me mother-in-law, eventually we got a house, which was a dump again. Then my husband was unemployed, that meant more beatings in for me, because whatever happened he used to take all his temper out on me. Then again I was expecting my other one, right? I've even had two miscarriages, where I've lost two when he's been beating me in. I would say 'what have I done?' I used to have everything spotless, do the cooking, do the cleaning, looking after the kids, making sure that everything's right for them. Life went on like that. Then eventually after thirteen years last March, I left him.

As life went on he didn't improve, he got worse you see. Sometimes people getting better don't they? He knew I'd had a hard life, childhood, but what did he do? He threw it back at me didn't he? 'Oh you can't go home. You're keeping your mum's reputation ain't you?' Right? Last year in March, something else must have happened at work, and he come in, just beat me in again. Broke me collarbone, right? When he was in his mood I used to really try and go upstairs and stay out of his way. I mean if I used to go upstairs he used to want to know why I'm upstairs.

That day he started saying things like 'oh, I'm a psycho, you not know I'm a psycho, I can kill you I can'. Get a knife out of the drawer and you know, actually have it there. 'You know, even if I do kill you, no one's going to know I killed you'. He broke my collarbone in February and then after it got better he was getting worse. He'd say 'when I come back make sure you get on your hands and knees and scrub them floorboards down there'. Then I was having a sort of a breakdown then. I was getting nervous. I was getting scared. I didn't know what was going on no more.

We had just moved into it, the house, in September, and I was really happy then, thinking 'oh I got me house' and it was my sort of dream house. It had a through lounge. I always wanted a separate dining room. We had a separate dining room. Then it had a kitchen, then you had a shed outside, then you had a toilet, and then you had another little shed to put your tools in. And then you had a garage and then you had a great big garden, then you had three bedrooms and then you had a bathroom. It was semi-detached. That was my dream house.

I was looking forward to the summer. I would put flowers in the garden, I would have them all the way round. Not knowing I wasn't going to live in the house. Right. So, as I say, bought the house in September, and then in March, when he was really getting worse, and I picks up the phone and goes to my brother 'oh, you always said you'd help me out and I need your help now, because I just can't take it no more. I'm coming home for good. I never want to come back to this place again. Just come for me please'.

I can't explain how I even felt. I didn't understand what I was going through. Terrified. Terrified. And I felt as if I don't want nothing on this earth no more. No energy, just lost. I feel dead now. I feel as if I'm just dead now. I don't want nothing in life. Then I left him, me brothers come for me. He [her husband] just sat in the room. He was just shocked. That's all. He went upstairs and we packed.

Then I'm in Kent and I'm thinking 'my kids, he's going to take my kids. He's going to come for me'. I'm too scared to go out the door even, down me mum's. That's it and I sit in me mum's house and I think 'what have I done? What *have* I done?' Left me house, left everything, ended up here. Maybe I'll just feel it today, be all right tomorrow. Sleep on it. Can't sleep. Next day, got to sort my kids out, go to my solicitor. She says I have to get an injunction out on him.

14

They can't take the kids away from me, he can't use any violence against you. So I get that. Send it off to him. And then we have a court case on May 1st. He doesn't arrive, he doesn't arrive.

The judge decided that, eh I've missed a lot out. He [her husband] put into the statements that her father was mental and she is as well [slight laugh]. And 'I don't approve of me kids living in that house because it's full of damp'. Well I get myself a council house, don't I? I get a council house within a month, down in Kent. And get me kids into school. I sort me money out, get the kids a doctor. Whatever they used to have interest in, football, swimming, cinema ... the things I did in them six months, they never even had before. The final court hearing decided he got the kids.

I can't live without the kids. I think I will go back. Me mum doesn't know I'm going to go back. Then I go back. Before we even set off he'd started again. I'm not bothered no more if I die. He was always coming in saying things like 'I'm going to kill you. I'm going to kill you. Get you back for what you've done to me. You know how much you've made me suffer when you've been away for six months?' You know, just driving me crazy. Beatings were getting worse. He just hated me. And I just got my bag and I just walked through the door.

I haven't seen the children since then, and that's a month now. I say I want to see them right? But I don't want them to know I'm in Wolverhampton, and I don't want to go to Preston. I want to see them but then my sister says that still there's a chance that he might follow you, and he might get to know where you are. I could have a share of the house if I want. But I don't want it, I'm just trying to make my life now. The only thing at the back of my mind is 'yeah one day I will drive down and I will see them'.

I've been here [in the hostel] for four weeks. And now I'm just really trying to get myself into college, get meself a career, going to learn to drive. Being here I can be myself now. There's only the pain of me kids, but apart from that I'm happy with life now. I am eventually happy with life. Everyone thinks you're happy because of his acting, and me not saying nothing to nobody. But who knows what's going on inside the house? Only me.

1 Researching homelessness

The homeless are the inhabitants of sub city, living in subterranean ways beneath the gloss and the affluence of post-modern cities. Street homeless lives are conducted in basement day-centres and in back alley-ways, while hostel-dwellers lead anonymous existences in towns and cities throughout the country. This sub city motif is a familiar one but does not convey the whole of its meaning, for beyond the well-documented urban situation lies the lesser-known rural homelessness. This takes us to the second meaning of sub city, the sense in which the countryside has been constructed as subordinate to the city, and its social problems thus rendered invisible (Lawrence, 1997; Milbourne, 1997). Finally, our concern is with the cultural adaptations and social organisation of homeless 'sub citizens', those who are socially marginal, economically disadvantaged and politically disenfranchised.

Even among the homeless themselves, all excluded to a greater or lesser degree from home, community and citizenship, some are less able than others to find a sense of belonging and identity. As we shall see in chapters four and six in particular, structural factors such as race and gender mediate individual experiences of home and homelessness, aside from the vagaries of personal biography and disposition.

The phenomenon of homelessness has fascinated successive generations of qualitative researchers, many of whom have engaged in extensive debates concerning the ethics, politics and morality of their enterprise. This chapter briefly reviews this research tradition, and is otherwise largely concerned with reflecting on my own role as an ethnographic researcher in relation to homeless people.

The research projects

The research on rural homelessness took place in Shropshire in 1992 and in North Wales in 1998: fifty focused interviews were conducted in Shropshire, and ten in-depth interviews in North Wales, along with some local archival research. This empirical work contributes to the rural case-studies presented in chapters six and two respectively, and the stories of two people in the

...ies study appeared in the prologue. These case-studies are
...t exploratory, given that rural homelessness is under-researched,
...vertheless they have something important to contribute to debates
...cerning the social ordering and regulation of space (Ching and Creed,
...97; Cloke et al, 1997).

The more extensive research was urban-based, and was conducted within
the ESRC-funded Three Cities Project. One hundred homeless young people
were interviewed in-depth in the cities of Manchester, Stoke-on-Trent and
Birmingham (plus two in Wolverhampton): four of these life-stories have
been related in the prologue, and aspects of many other lives appear in
chapters four, five and six. A range of homeless situations was investigated,
including hostel-dwellers, squatters, new age travellers and the street
homeless. The majority of these young people were contacted via agencies
working with the homeless - including hostels, day-centres and *Big Issue*
offices - and a minority were contacted directly on the streets in order to
include those who subsist outside of the homelessness circuit.

Interviews were also conducted with representatives from an extensive
range of statutory and voluntary agencies: hostel managers and day-centre
staff; staff in *Big Issue* offices and on soup-runs; police and probation
officers; social and youth workers; housing and social security officials; drug
and alcohol advisers; pressure group coordinators and many others. Over a
period of two years, extensive observation (sometimes participant but more
often not) was conducted of homelessness in these three cities. This is the
method - perhaps the most problematic as well as the most productive - that
is addressed in the three scenarios below.

The Three Cities Project took place at a time when street homelessness
was high on the political agenda, with particular attention being directed to
the associated incivilities of begging and sleeping rough (Hunter, 1985).
The Criminal Justice and Public Order Act 1994 was passing through
parliament and both Government and Opposition were fulminating against
those modern folk devils, beggars and new age travellers. Few could fail to
be aware that the face of 'new' homelessness was becoming ever more
youthful and desperate.

Recent economic and social policy initiatives had included radical and
detrimental changes to the welfare benefit system for young people (Carlen
1996); reduced entitlement to rehousing on the part of the homeless; and the
instigation of the Rough Sleepers' Initiative, first in London and then in
other English and Scottish towns and cities (Randall and Brown, 1993). On
the criminal justice front, high numbers of beggars were being prosecuted
under the 1824 Vagrancy Act, while police responses alternated between a
reluctance to arrest homeless people for what were essentially status
offences, and the undertaking of periodic special operations designed to
clear the city streets of beggars and rough sleepers. The evolution and
provisions of the 1824 Vagrancy Act are examined further in chapter two,
while chapter six takes up the question of police responses to street homeless
people.

The project set out to investigate from an ethnographic perspective
criminalisation, victimisation and lawbreaking among the homeless
population (Carlen, 1996; Wardhaugh, 1996; Wardhaugh, 1999). Within

these general empirical and methodological parameters, each m̶
team had a different research role to develop, both in the field and
to one another. The research assistant was appointed in the second
the project and, as a streetwise man who shared many aspects of
culture with the subjects of his research, he soon developed his own distin̶
research role. As a junior researcher (having completed a Masters degree,
but not yet registered for a doctorate) he was accountable to both the other
members of the team, and received general academic supervision from Pat
Carlen and more specific fieldwork training from myself.

The roles of the co-directors and joint grant-holders on the project were
somewhat different. As professor and head of department, Pat Carlen was
involved in a range of other academic activities and therefore engaged in
general oversight rather than direct involvement in fieldwork. As a full-time
senior researcher on the project my time was spent in intensive fieldwork, in
day-to-day supervision of the research assistant, and in detailed planning and
development of the project.

In terms of funding, we were invited to resubmit our initial proposal to
the Economic and Social Research Council, and were successful with our
second, somewhat smaller-scale version. We were confident that we could
construct, as requested by the funding body, a successful project around two
research workers rather than three as originally requested, but an issue of
great concern to us was the question of making payments to interviewees.
Our initial request for the (we thought) modest amount of £1,000 was
rejected on the grounds of lack of precedent, although one of us (Carlen) had
made such payments under a previous grant from the same funding body.

It was our strong political and ethical belief that socially and
economically vulnerable participants in our study should be paid for their
time, and so we contrived in a number of ways to make such payments
possible, sometimes in cash and sometimes in kind (food and cigarettes).
We understood the possible objection that we were therefore 'buying'
people's stories, but were able in practice to ensure willing participation on
the part of potential interviewees before the question of payment was raised.
In paying homeless people for their time we were reversing the more usual
emphasis on the researcher entering the world of the researched, and instead
brought them a little way into 'our' world, with its emphasis on the dignity of
employment and economic reward for labour.

Personal biography

Many ethnographers talk about having 'paid their dues' by virtue of their
participation in the physical privations and social indignities of
homelessness, and thus of having earned the right to conduct their research
and subsequently to tell their stories. Harper, for example, presented himself
'with the outside trappings of a skid row man' in order to gain rich
qualitative data as an 'inside observer' (1979:26). He recognised the ethical
dilemmas involved in such covert participant observation, but failed to
anticipate the dangers of 'going native':

; and more integrated into the lifestyle, I realised that it
/e to me to experience the life of my informants than it
)cuments about it (Harper, 1979:27).

s not these dangers that deterred me from adopting
; a research technique, but rather some personal and
s. My own experience of homelessness might have
hat perhaps I had already 'paid my dues' and therefore
/e myself in this way. Encounters with homelessness
'orms within my personal biography, including several
stel as an infant and a period of 'hidden homelessness' in
later childhood - an episode when our small nuclear family (mother, brother
and myself) lived in one household with several members of our extended
family, while awaiting rehousing.

However, to use such aspects of personal biography (either past
experiences of homelessness or present attempts to enter the social world of
homelessness) in order to claim some particular authenticity for one's
research seems to me to be of limited validity, in both personal and
intellectual terms. Personal biography is of course important in bringing us
to the point of conducting our fieldwork, and will inevitably influence the
quality of our interactions within the field. In my case early experiences
undoubtedly affected my motivation to engage in homelessness research, as
well as informing the nature and quality of my fieldwork. Nevertheless,
leaving aside the tramp authors who may or may not have been homeless,
researchers of homelessness are in the privileged position of having a safe
and comfortable home to which to return, either after the end of their day's
work or following a period spent undercover as a 'homeless person'. I
believe it is essential to acknowledge the material and social differences that
exist between the researcher and the researched, and thus to recognise the
limits that necessarily exist in terms of 'our' entering into 'their' world.

Homelessness research

Social scientific exploration of homelessness has a long history, dating back
in Britain as far as the Elizabethan rogue pamphleteers who established what
some commentators have interpreted as a proto-sociological perspective, and
who certainly pioneered qualitative and ethnographic approaches to the
study of vagrancy (Harman, 1566; Dekker, 1608; Aydelotte, 1913; Judges,
1930; Kinney, 1990). This tradition was later developed by the Victorian
and Edwardian 'social explorers': the philanthropists, novelists and social
scientists who regularly went undercover in their investigations of the social
world of homelessness, and many of whose methods and perspectives were
to influence subsequent generations of ethnographers (Dickens, 1853; Higgs,
1906; Chesterton, 1928; Beresford, 1979). Chapter three examines this
literature of homelessness and crime in some depth.

From the early twentieth century onwards, the geographical centre of
such enquiries shifted from Britain to North America, with the denizens of
the Main Stem and Skid Row quickly becoming established as a major focus

of interest for sociological and criminological ethnographers. In the years up to 1965 alone, more than 150 North American studies were published about Skid Row, that real yet symbolic location that came to epitomise marginality, deviance and social exclusion (Wallace, 1965; Russell, 1991).

Perhaps the most famous of these early American ethnographers was Nels Anderson (1923), whose Chicago School study of 'hobohemia' proved to be definitive in terms of both theory and methodology. Anderson departed from the conventions of inter-war sociological theory that defined marginal people as dysfunctional deviations from social and economic norms, instead developing a detailed and sympathetic account of the complexities and intricacies of hobo life. Such knowledge derived from his own time spent on the road: 'for a number of years Anderson had not been a participant observer and bona fide sociologist: instead he had been an observing participant and bona fide hobo' (Watson, 1997:x). Moral and ethical considerations notwithstanding, such extended periods spent 'going native' undoubtedly served to produce material that is rich in qualitative detail.

The drive to seek ethnographic authenticity by going undercover, while rarely adopted for such extended periods as was the case with Anderson, was nevertheless a significant part of the North American qualitative tradition of homelessness research from the 1920s until the 1970s, after which time it began to decline in popularity as a research technique (Allsop, 1967; McSheehy, 1979; Vander Kooi, 1973; Wiseman, 1973). Those contemporary ethnographers who have attempted to go undercover have encountered both psychological and ethical difficulties:

> Psychologically I knew I was not homeless ... yet I ended my participation after two nights ... because I was becoming deeply depressed ... and I began to understand how one's identity can be lost. I also knew that a homeless woman might need my bed (Russell 1991:28).

Perhaps times had changed in that researchers were by now more willing to admit to such difficulties, or perhaps as a woman Russell took a different view of the streets. Certainly, female ethnographers have been more likely to acknowledge the psychic and physical dangers of homelessness, and have been less drawn to the romantic imagery of the open road than their male counterparts (Crouse, 1986; Garrett and Bahr, 1976; Harper, 1982; Golden 1992).

The majority of studies up until the 1970s focused on one dimension of Skid Row life above all others: the consumption of alcohol. Although excessive consumption was to be found only among a minority of the homeless, this nevertheless came to serve as a signifier both of the social deviance and the psychological alienation of the denizens of Skid Row. Despite such a focus on marginality and alienation, the criminological dimension of most such studies remained implicit, with only a few adopting an explicit empirical focus on crime and deviance (see for example Bittner, 1967; Rose, 1965, 1997; Spradley, 1970).

Rose provides an ethnographic and ethnonomic account of Skid Row in Denver, Colorado, leading a team of researchers, one of whom 'played the

21

role of a bum' during the course of the investigations (Rose, 1965:3). Unusually for its time, this study of Larimer Street focused on the agents of social control as well as on the men living in this 'unattached society'. Rose added his distinctive methods of analysing natural language to the already diverse and well-developed tradition of homelessness research, emphasising the need to understand social worlds from the inside by means of first-hand accounts. For Rose language was not simply the means by which social interaction took place, it was the very essence of such interaction. Consequently his report contains extensive narrative accounts taken from the field, accounts such as the 'poignant story of survival' told to Rose by Johnny O'Leary.

Dedicated to 'my friend the tramp', Spradley's (1970) classic ethnographic study of 'urban nomads' is one of the few within this empirical and methodological genre to focus specifically on criminal justice dimensions of Skid Row life. Spradley documents the complex social rituals that take place over time and in space to define individuals as 'tramps' or 'bums' and thus render them liable to arrest for what they are rather than for what they do. The ethnographic power of this text centres around its vivid descriptions of the stages involved in 'making the bucket', that is, being arrested and incarcerated in the 'drunk tank' as a tramp.

In Britain during this period, work on homelessness was mostly written in a social documentary or journalistic style, and was motivated primarily by an agenda of social concern and social change (Deakin and Willis, 1976; Erlam and Brown, 1976; Wallich-Clifford, 1974; Wilkinson, 1981; Sandford, 1971; 1976). With only isolated exceptions (see for example Archard, 1979), an academic ethnographic tradition of homelessness research did not become established in Britain during the second half of the twentieth century, and therefore the present project referred in methodological terms to a mainly North American corpus of work (Russell, 1991; Golden, 1992; Snow and Anderson, 1993; Wagner, 1993).

A few British ethnographic researchers were working contemporaneously with us, although they did not necessarily adopt a criminological focus (see for example Hutson and Liddiard, 1994). In North America the focus shifted during the 1980s towards a mainly quantitative perspective, with an emphasis on a census and survey approach to the enumeration and demographic profiling of the homeless population (Baumann et al, 1985; Roth et al, 1985; Rossi et al, 1987; Lee, 1989). By the late 1980s and early 1990s, however, a small but healthy qualitative tradition had been re-established, and it was this tradition that was to inform and inspire our work (Glasser, 1988; Kozol, 1988; Golden, 1992; Snow and Anderson, 1993).

Participant observation

The predominant method adopted by qualitative homelessness researchers has been participant observation, a significant proportion of which has been covert in nature, although authors often prefer more romantic descriptions such as 'going undercover' or 'taking the role of a bum'. Without entering into the extensive methodological debates that surround participant observation, it seems reasonable to state in general terms that research roles adopted may vary from complete participant to complete observer, with most researchers occupying a position somewhere between these two extremes (Junker, 1960; Gregor, 1977; Pollert, 1981; Hammersley and Atkinson, 1995).

A second dimension relates to degrees of overtness or covertness during the observation process. In my experience 'overt' and 'covert' should be understood as points on a continuum rather than as polar opposites, and perhaps most such fieldwork can best be described as semi-overt (or semi-covert, depending on whether you like to think of your glass as half-full or half-empty) participant observation (Gilbert, 1993; Mason, 1996; O'Connell Davidson and Layder, 1994). Taken together, these two continua (from covert to overt and from participation to observation) provide innumerable potential positions to be adopted by the ethnographic researcher. The following scenarios describe some of the research roles I adopted within the Three Cities Project, varying from that of semi-overt, semi-participant observer in scenes one and two, to covert complete observer in scene three.

Scene one

Setting: a day centre for the homeless in central Manchester, entered by means of narrow steps leading down from a side street which borders a canal (see Figure 1.1). A few hundred yards away are the busy rail and coach terminals serving the city, and a short walk further takes you to the main shopping mall. Few shoppers, tourists or business people come down this street and if they did they would not notice the centre as there is no sign advertising its presence. Once inside the centre it is warm and noisy, full of people talking, eating, playing pool or just sitting and staring into space. Food and drink is provided at regular intervals and at low cost, shower and laundry facilities are available, and users of the centre may seek advice from staff and share conversation among themselves.

Time spent in this particular day centre proved to be central to the research process both in the establishment of research roles and in the development of research questions and theoretical perspectives. Participant observation took place in a more or less overt fashion, with staff and some key informants consenting to the research, although it would have proven to be very difficult (and probably intrusive) to seek individual permission from each of the dozens of people using the centre over the course of several days of observation (Hammersley and Atkinson, 1995). A formula that worked in this situation was to seek formal permission from the central characters in this particular drama, and then to negotiate various roles and relationships with the minor players. For example, I was able to discuss my research agenda with one forthright young man who asked me directly what I was doing, while it seemed more suitable to accept the role of volunteer helper allocated to me by some of the older users of the centre, a role with which we were all comfortable. In practice, the limited adoption of the tasks of a

23

Figure 1.1 Cardboard city: day centre for the homeless, Manchester.
Photograph taken by the author.

volunteer (for example helping to serve meals) helped me to overcome the awkwardness inherent in conducting research in social settings within which there is no clearly defined role to be adopted.

Days spent documenting the detail of interactions within the centre as well as observing the wider picture led to the emergence of a series of research questions around the use of social space. As an observer, it seemed to me that people entered the centre in waves of movement that were largely determined by temporal factors such as mealtimes, and that they then proceeded to make use of the physical space of the centre in ways that were both regular and socially meaningful. One notable pattern was that young men tended to dominate the prime space adjacent to the small staff office, while women and older men both practically and metaphorically faded into the background. More sociable members congregated in the 'front regions' around the kitchen serving-area and thus received the greater share of staff attention, while lone men and women sat towards the back of the centre, apparently content in their occupation of marginal places (Goffman, 1971).

Day centres such as this one can be understood as 'free spaces' within a cityscape that is generally hostile to marginal groups, in that users of the centre are generally free from interventions by the police or by members of the public, but this should not be taken to mean that this is unregulated space (Wagner, 1993). Such centres are subject to their own forms of social and spatial ordering, such as differential occcupation and use of space according to factors such as age and gender. Furthermore, they are also part of a wider nexus of socio-spatial relations by virtue of their belonging to a network of such locations on the homelessness circuit. For example, it became clear from my wider series of observations of life on the 'circuit' that at least some street homeless people moved in a regular diurnal pattern between day centres, and from day centres to soup-runs and back again, and that in this way their lives were systematically regulated in both temporal and spatial terms (Wardhaugh, 1996).

Major theoretical questions around the use of space began to be developed on the basis of these observations, and in particular queries around the binary division of space along two axes: public and private, and prime and marginal (Lofland, 1973; Snow and Anderson, 1993; see chapter six for an exploration of these questions). A central 'puzzlement' was how significant numbers of stigmatised and marginal street people could effectively disappear from the city streets, and at least part of the answer seemed to lie in the existence of interstitial, marginal locations such as day centres within prime city centre space (Hammersley and Atkinson, 1995).

Scene two

Setting: the same day centre at night. Situated on the borderline between Cardboard city and the red-light district, the centre is used by working-girls in the evenings, and is supported at this time by a separate agency: different staff, different clientele, different ambience. The researcher's aim was to talk to any of the working girls who might be homeless, and she musters her courage to approach them 'cold' on the street. Staff have said that she may interview them in the centre, but must make the initial contact herself as they do not want to become known as 'the agency that administers questionnaires to homeless people'. Things do not go exactly according to plan ...

> JW: [Nervous and trying to act streetwise, introduces herself to two women standing on the street corner outside the centre, and makes some general conversation with them. Wishing to make contact with homeless women working as prostitutes, she wonders about the ethics of assuming the nature of someone's profession from their socio-spatial behaviour.]
>
> I'm hoping to talk to some homeless people in connection with some work that I'm doing ... do you know anyone who might be interested?
>
> [Wonders whether they will recognise this as a not very subtle ploy to enlist their own co-operation as potential interviewees.]
>
> Two women: The homeless youngsters hang around over in Piccadilly Gardens, you can always find someone there at this time of night [9pm]. We're homeless ourselves [they look at each other] ... we wouldn't mind talking to you but we're busy just now, we need one more punter each and then we can go, 'cause we've got things to do tonight. But we can talk to you some other time ... Look, there's Jimmy, he's homeless, do you want us to shout over to him, he knows everyone and I'm sure he'll help you.

Jimmy did indeed prove to be helpful, not only in agreeing to be interviewed himself, but in introducing me to people congregating around the Piccadilly Garden soup-run, several of whom agreed to be interviewed later that evening in the centre. It is impossible for the participant observer in such locations to feel safe and contained, or for their work to be planned and predictable. However, it is essential to balance the potentially dangerous nature of such work and questions of personal safety against the drive to conduct research, something rarely mentioned within the often macho world of homeless ethnographers (but see Garrett and Bahr, 1976). In this particular instance I did feel relatively safe, partly because daylight lingered far into the summer evening, partly because I had made myself familiar with the contours and boundaries of Cardboard city, and partly because I was working for some of the time within the staffed base of the centre. Nevertheless, I cannot think of any other circumstances in which I would agree to wander through the city with a group of young men that I had only just met, nor where I would not resent the role of protector that they adopted in relation to me.

On this occasion, interviews and participant observation shaded into one another as research techniques, in the sense that formal, tape-recorded interviews were conducted within the centre amidst a series of other activities (Hammersley and Atkinson, 1995). A degree of privacy was maintained by choosing a quiet corner for conversation while the other men played bar football or 'had a brew', and a steady stream of women came into the centre in search of tea, condoms, advice and conversation. Nevertheless, during interviews we were in full view (although not necessarily within hearing distance) of several other people, and we ourselves were participants in the ongoing life of the centre.

This was to prove to be an important factor when towards midnight two men arrived and aggressively demanded to be interviewed for payment. This interlude can be read in two ways: they were drunk and abusive men threatening a female researcher (and therefore they were exploitative); or they were needy individuals disturbed by the introduction of a cash exchange into the homelessness circuit (and they were therefore potentially exploited). I think that this situation may be read in both ways: that is, both the researcher and the researched were potentially vulnerable as a result of the complex and unstable balance of power that existed between them. In practical terms the important thing was to defuse a situation that was potentially dangerous or disturbing to all those present, and this was achieved by the quiet offering of cigarettes and a small amount of money (about half the standard amount paid to interviewees) to the two new arrivals. The central dilemma was that payments to interviewees undoubtedly eased the making of contacts on the streets, but at the same time money proved to be a potentially explosive ingredient when introduced from outside into street homeless culture.

A further significant theoretical concern emerged from this fieldwork episode in that the very different purposes to which this centre was put at night and by day highlighted the importance of time as a social variable within the lives of street homeless people. Questions around space had already begun to be addressed, but now a temporal dimension could be added to an analysis of the regulation of street life (Murray, 1986; Rowe and Wolch, 1990). Later pursuit of this theme began to reveal the ways in which the daily subsistence round of the street homeless person is structured over time and within space and this theme is addressed further in chapter six (Wardhaugh, 1996).

Scene three

In an ongoing scenario that unfolds over many months, the researcher spends time exploring the contours of Cardboard city and its neighbouring 'urban villages'. She wanders down back alley-ways and under canal bridges, noting places where people might sleep at night or by day. Sometimes pieces of cardboard or blankets are left out to mark someone's patch, and on winter days the attraction of the hot-air vents of the restaurants of Chinatown becomes obvious. Both official and unofficial locations used by the homeless are carefully noted, and gradually the social and spatial boundaries of Cardboard city are mapped. These boundaries are clear but not static, in that there is a dynamic interaction between Cardboard city and its three neighbouring districts: the red-light area, Chinatown and the Gay village, all places where street homeless people work, eat and sleep. Observations are made of the interactions between street people and other users of the city centre: of hostile or sympathetic exchanges between Big Issue vendors and members of the public, or the occasional police questioning of people engaged in begging.

27

Figure 1.2 Cardboard city: sleeping by the canal, Minshull Street bridge, Manchester.
Photograph taken by Chris Carter.

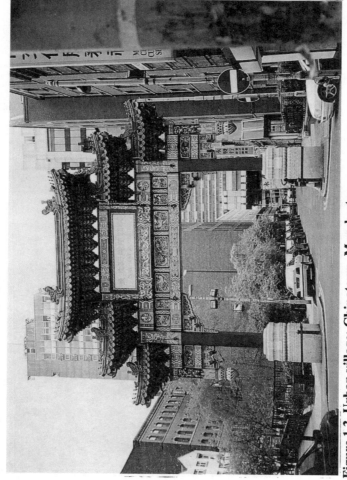

Figure 1.3 Urban village: Chinatown, Manchester.
Photograph taken by Chris Carter.

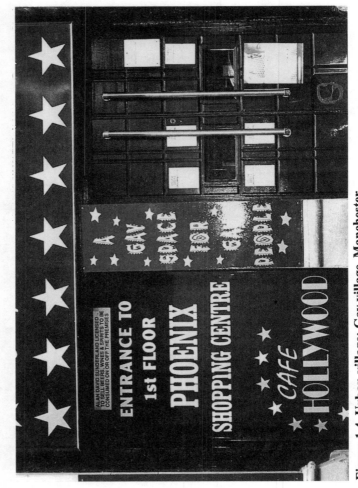

Figure 1.4 Urban village: Gay village, Manchester.
Photograph taken by Chris Carter.

Theoretical questions around the social use of space that arose from scenes one and two led to the adoption of a specific research role in scene three: that of covert, complete observer. By this I mean that no-one else in the settings observed was aware of my presence as a researcher, and there was no degree of social interaction other than that shared by passers-by. Inspired in various ways by social ecological, symbolic interactionist, socio-geographical and Foucauldian analyses of the cityscape, my intention was to document the cognitive maps used by street homeless people in their efforts at daily subsistence, and to gain along the way a sense of the *genius loci* of Cardboard city (Gans, 1962; Pocock and Hudson, 1978; Davis, 1990; Shields, 1991; Sibley, 1995).

In terms of methods the choice was clear: covert observations of the spaces and places used by homeless people would allow for the development of a social cartography of Cardboard city in a way that would have been complicated by an overt or semi-overt participant role. Quite simply, an obvious research presence (even if this were possible to negotiate within the ever-changing tableau of street life) would alter the nature of interactions and behaviours taking place. However, for me the role of covert observer was both unfamiliar and ethically questionable.

Looking to academic precedent for guidance on the ethics of covert observation in public settings, Lofland's (1973) excellent micro-sociological study of social interactions in public places, based largely on visual observations conducted through a window looking out on to city streets, appeared to offer reassurance that this was an acceptable technique. However, her study was based on observations of shoppers, business people and commuters, people for whom the public-private distinction was of relevance. If they enter into public space, the argument reasonably might go, then their actions within such space are by definition public in nature and therefore open to general observation.

For street homeless people, however, there is no such clear separation between public and private domains: their whole daily round is carried out in public places, and they have no private space to which they may retreat, although they may contrive temporarily to define some places as semi-private. My observations were partly of general public space (shopping malls, coach stations, shops and cafes) but they also inevitably intruded into private or semi-private lives: for example, glimpsing 'back-region' behaviours such as personal grooming or stumbling across someone's bedding in an alley-way (Goffman, 1959). The usual conventions of seeking permission to conduct observations seemed impossible to apply within this context (who exactly would give such permission?), yet the ethical dilemma remained difficult to resolve. I wondered whether it was possible to avoid being a 'research tourist' or '*flâneur*', someone who voyeuristically enjoys their time spent as an observer without having any substantial contribution to make (Wilson, 1995; Cloke and Little, 1997).

As is often the case with such ethnographic research, no clear-cut answers were forthcoming, and the resolution achieved in this instance relied on pragmatism as much as on abstract principles. In the end, guidelines for research practice in this type of situation were formulated, based both on my ethical beliefs and research experience over an extended period of time.

These guidelines included a commitment to be as unobtrusive and non-invasive as possible during observations; to maintain acceptable levels of personal space between myself and those observed; to conduct visual but not aural observations, on the grounds that the latter were more invasive than the former; and to respect the usual research conventions concerning confidentiality and anonymity. Above all, the most important objective (successfully achieved I think) was not to violate the already constantly threatened privacy and dignity of people living on the streets.

Conclusion

An ethical code adapted from the medical profession might serve well within social ethnography: 'if you can do no good, at least do no harm'. Within the tradition of homelessness research in particular, with its tendency to romanticise its subjects and to observe them in a covert fashion, this principle is of particular relevance. The Three Cities Project was pioneering within the British context of such research in its adoption of an ethnographic perspective and in its criminological empirical and theoretical focus. An ethnographic approach promises the production of richly-detailed fieldwork materials, but brings with it also a range of ethical, moral and political considerations. In recognition of the complexity of street homeless lives, a variety of participant, observer and interviewer roles were adopted during the collection of data, and in so doing a number of ethical dilemmas were encountered and perhaps resolved.

The internal and moral coherence of the project cannot be separated from the wider social and political context within which street homeless people were being demonised and criminalised by politicians and the media, a process that was itself a major focus for our research. Just as research and ethical questions were closely related, so too was there an intimate connection between theory and method. For example, 'puzzlements' about the social use of space by homeless people arose from fieldwork observations, and this interest in turn led to the adoption of a role I would not have envisaged at the outset: that of covert observer. The relation between theory and method can thus be said to be cyclical rather than linear, and often to develop in an organic rather than mechanical fashion.

Chapters four, five and six develop the substantive arguments arising from this dynamic tension between theory and method, but first the next two chapters provide a discussion of the legislative and literary contexts of our discussion of homelessness and crime.

2 From vagabondage to homelessness

Laws do not arise full-grown children of the dragon's teeth. They do not enjoy an uncomplicated and unproblematic relationship with the settings and intentions of their original drafting. Rather, they undergo natural histories whose unwindings shape them in ways never anticipated by their first authors (Rock, 1974:10).

..the general rule of all England is to whip and punish the wandering beggars (seventeenth century pamphleteer; in O'Connor, 1963:40).

The journey from vagabondage to homelessness is a long one, beginning with medieval regulation of 'idle and valiant' beggars, and ending in the late twentieth century with conflicting welfare and criminal justice discourses on the nature of homelessness. On this journey we move back and forth between an understanding of homelessness as a social issue to its definition as a law-and-order problem. Such movement is cyclical rather than linear, with discourses shifting and changing with the ebb and flow of social, economic and political tides. At the same time, we are able to trace the emergence and development of discourses on the condition itself, from the description of vagrancy, roguery and vagabondage in medieval to Victorian times, to the rough sleepers and homeless persons terminology of contemporary legislation and welfare provision.

The first part of this chapter traces legislative responses to vagrancy and homelessness, from medieval to contemporary times. Legislation often outlives the original context within which it was drafted and developed, and this is nowhere more true than in the case of vagrancy and homelessness. Attention is often drawn to the survival of the 1824 Vagrancy Act into the late twentieth century, but it is often forgotten that this Act itself replaced and rationalised 27 earlier vagrancy acts (Rose, 1988). In this way, layer upon layer of legislation impacts on contemporary lives.

The second part of the chapter consists of a case-study of North Wales, based on local archival material as well as academic sources. Despite modern representations of homelessness as an urban phenomenon, historically much vagrancy has either been located in rural areas, or else has had its economic origins in rural impoverishment. This historical examination of vagrancy in North Wales serves both to uncover this largely forgotten history of rural homelessness, and to provide a starting point for the analysis of contemporary rural homelessness and crime which is taken up in chapter six.

Regulating vagrancy

From holy poverty to idle beggars

The story of the regulation of the vagrant and the beggar begins in the High Middle Ages, when around 1300 CE Pauline Christianity, with its emphasis on each person earning their own passage through life, began to replace the earlier Franciscan idealisation of 'holy poverty'. Early and early medieval Christianity was not alone in its ideological reverence for the poor, sharing this with other world religions such as Islam and Buddhism. However, it is possible to detect within each of these traditions a deep ambivalence towards the practice of almsgiving to the wandering stranger. Charity is accepted by both parties as a duty and as a right, but the act of giving serves also to neutralise the fearfulness and sense of danger inspired by the placeless Other, while at the same time rendering the recipient dependent and therefore less than equal, a non-person or non-citizen (Golden, 1992).

The first statute restricting the traditional almsgiving function of the monasteries was passed in 1274, on the grounds that they were 'overcharged and sore grieved' by the weight of such demands on their resources (Chambliss, 1964). This statute was designed to regulate claims for relief made by travellers rather than to prevent vagrancy as such, but it is significant in signalling the beginning of radical changes in attitudes towards begging and almsgiving. During the first half of the fourteenth century, a concern began to grow about begging among the able-bodied poor, with the notion of the soon to be infamous 'idle beggar' becoming increasingly well-established. These fears culminated in the statute of 1349 that decreed imprisonment as the punishment for those donating alms to 'idle' but 'valiant' beggars. This is an interesting and exceptional instance of the almsgiver rather than the beggar being subject to punishment. The 'impotent' poor could continue to receive alms, but only if remaining at their present residence or place of birth: the drive to prevent wandering thus became clearly established in law.

These changing attitudes to begging arose at least in part from the social and economic upheavals that were threatening to lead to the breakdown of the feudal system. The devastation of the population following the Black Death and the general drift of former serfs and villeins to the newly-developing towns and cities served to depopulate rural areas, with wide-ranging implications for a social system based on stable patterns of land ownership and labour. Legislation such as that passed in 1351 sought to prevent the free movement of people from countryside to town, and to maintain the availability of cheap agricultural labour.

Punishing the vagrant body

Having been established in times of cri⌐'
persisted into the later medieval period, ir
as they singularly failed to alter the co⌐'
of labour from rural to urban area⌐
population, and the steady breakdown⌐
legislation was developed during the pe⌐
frequently failed to implement existing legi⌐
was a significant gap, then, between the harsh⌐
practical implementation of the judicial and pena⌐
and beggars.

Nevertheless, it is important to note the at least s⌐
statutes that provided for 15 days imprisonment (136⌐
(1388), and banishment from town (1495) for those con⌐
Furthermore, there was a remarkable degree of local discret⌐
before the centralisation of state power and authority, and
vagrants and beggars in certain areas of the country would
subjected to harsher physical penalties than their counterparts else⌐
statute in 1383 formalised this discretionary treatmant of vagabonds, .
that local justices and sheriffs were authorised to 'do upon such feitor⌐
vagabonds that which to them best shall seem by the laws' (O'Conn⌐
1963:40). A series of controls of the physical body of the offender
(containment, exclusion and humiliation) were thus established, a not at all
unusual response at this time. What has been notable in the control of
vagrancy - and later homelessness - is that such physical punishments have
rarely been accompanied or replaced in later times by attempts to reform the
mind.

Criminalising beggars and vagrants

> Vagrancy is perhaps the classic crime of status, the social crime *par
> excellence*. Offenders were arrested not because of their actions, but
> because of their position in society (Beier, 1985:xxii).

The early sixteenth century is notable for two developments in the vagrancy
legislation: levels of punishment were briefly reduced during the period
1503-30, and the condition of vagrancy became more clearly criminalised,
as distinct from being understood as a rather undifferentiated social problem.
The statute of 1530 established unprecedentedly harsh punishment for
vagrancy, and identified the undeserving beggar or vagrant as those
impostors who only pretended to be poor and homeless: those to be punished
most severely included those 'using divers and subtil crafty and unlawful
games and plays' in order to beg for alms or to avoid legitimate employment
(Chambliss, 1976:243).

Although the branding of vagrants had technically been allowed since as
early as 1361, it was not frequently enforced until after the statute passed in
1604 (Beier, 1985). The mutilations (as well as the use of beatings and
pillories) that followed the 1530 Act were therefore significant in

35

permanently disfiguring and stigmatic punishment, one
et the vagrant apart from society. This was compounded by the
in 1563 of regulations concerning the badging of beggars.
the definition of vagrancy as a felony, one punishable by death.
e year an early 'sus' law was introduced, with the carceral net
ened to include those suspected of vagabondage: 'any ruffians ...
all wander, loiter, or idle use themselves and play the vagabonds'
liss, 1976:245). The charge of 'playing the vagabond' has echoed
the centuries, with contested claims being made today on the one
y impoverished youth who display 'homeless and hungry' signs while
ng, and hostile politicians on the other who call for 'zero tolerance' of
ressive beggars, winos and squeegee merchants' (Jack Straw, Shadow
me Secretary, September 1995).

By mid-century further categories were incorporated into the definition of
agabond'. Perhaps the most surprising inclusion was of those 'lurking in
any house' as well as those 'wandering by the highway side, or in streets,
cities, towns or villages, not applying themselves to some honest labour...'
(1547 statute, cited in Chambliss, 1976:246). Given that a 'vagabond' was by
both etymological origin and common understanding a 'wanderer', the
inclusion of private domestic space within the ambit of official regulation
was a significant departure indeed. It signalled the shift in understanding of
vagrancy from something one does to something one is, that is, a shift in
emphasis from behaviour to identity. It marked also the intrusion of official
regulation into the private sphere. The Criminal Justice and Public Order Act
1994 was to echo this theme more than four centuries later in its attempt to
regulate behaviour within private spaces (e.g. squatting) as well as to control
the use of public places (e.g. new age travellers).

During the latter half of the century, a period that also saw the
codification of the Elizabethan Poor Laws, the punishment of the vagrant
body had reached its peak, along with a radical disenfranchisement of
vagabonds and beggars. According to a 1547 statute, the evidence of two
witnesses was sufficient to identify someone as a vagabond, who was then
liable to be branded with a 'v' on the chest and enslaved for two years to the
person intercepting them: subsequent absconding was punishable by the
branding of an 's' on the forehead, along with permanent enslavement
(Chambliss, 1976).

By 1571, legislation emphasised the dangerousness of vagrants, with legal
discourse shifting from the simple (deviant but not dangerous) category of
'vagabond' to the criminality implicit in the new compound term 'rogue and
vagabond'. 'Rogue' was a word of cant origin new to the sixteenth century,
and was used to describe a newly-emerging concept: that vagabonds were
not only feckless but also dishonest and inclined towards criminality. This
new term was quickly incorporated into official discourse, and contributed to
the development of new forms of regulation. Chapter 17 of the 1571 statute
clearly expressed the fears engendered by the Tudor moral panic over
beggars, vagrants and vagabonds:

> Whereas divers licentious persons wander up and down ... to the great
> terror of her majesty's true subjects, the impeachment of her laws, and

the disturbance of the peace and tranquillitv
1976:247).

Criminal justice responses to such fear
vagrants, along with frequent departure
The Vagrancy Act of 1495 enabled ur'
place, searches that were to continue
seventeenth centuries. Major nat'
periods of social and political unrest,
1632-39. Police initiatives during the 19.
in Stoke-on-Trent are modern attempts
contemporary vagrant: the homeless perso.
disenfranchisement of vagrants was compounde
martial law (late 16th-early 17th centuries) and to sun.
early 17th centuries). In Tudor and Stuart times, summa.
were frequently held out of court by constables a.
administratively convenient and economic of effort and re.
undertakings represented an extension of state powers, and a.
locally-powerful to try offenders or suspected offenders at will (Bei.
Pound, 1971).

Imprisonment was relatively infrequently used as a punishment 1.
vagrancy: being an expensive form of regulation it was usually confined to
those vagrants deemed to be felonious. By the end of the sixteenth century,
vagrants were being sent to the new bridewells, but were seldom detained
long: they were usually whipped and quickly released rather than being
subjected to the new reformative regimes (Beier, 1985). Contemporary
accounts suggest that vagrants feared the houses of correction far more than
they did the gaols.

The early modern revolving door

The medieval attempt to confine beggars to their parishes of current
residence or of origin was echoed by the 1662 Law of Settlement and
Removal which required that the dependent poor be returned to their original
place of settlement if they were to receive relief. Many were unable to
establish their places of origin, or were unwilling to return there, and so
entered into a perpetual round of 'passing' from parish to parish, each as
unwilling as the last to provide poor relief.

By the end of the seventeenth century, a century of developing capitalism
and the emergence of the Protestant work ethic, half the population of
England were poor (either dependent or semi-dependent) and there were an
estimated 30,000 vagrants in a population of five-and-a-half million (Laslett,
1965). Established under the Elizabethan Poor Law of 1601, the workhouse
system remained relatively under-developed during the seventeenth century,
with an emphasis on outdoor relief for the majority, and some indoor relief
for the able-bodied poor. The gradual incorporation of the poor into the
workhouse system during the late 17th and early 18th centuries was
consolidated by the abolition of outdoor relief in 1723.

uses confined the poor and the homeless alongside the
the insane, and subjected all to regimes of work, discipline and
gain, such developments represented an attempt to control and
mentous social and economic change, in this instance the changes
ing the agricultural revolution. The workhouse system provided a
eans for controlling the poor and placeless. First, halting their
g served to relieve the fears of danger and disruption experienced
more affluent. Second, confining the most obvious manifestations of
read poverty to institutions helped to alleviate unwelcome conflict
en ascendant capitalist impulses towards individualism and
petitiveness, and still influential Christian traditions of almsgiving and
rity (Golden, 1992).

Consolidation and rationalisation of the criminal law

The late 16th to late 18th centuries was a period within which vagrancy
legislation remained largely unchanged, and it was not until the late 18th
century that the categories of vagrant and vagabond once again began to be
expanded and refined. Even then, there was little change to the spirit of the
vagrancy legislation which continued to criminalise the poor and the
homeless. The major development was a further widening of the carceral
net, to include ever more diverse populations within the definition of
'vagrant'. In 1743 for example, people gathering alms or charitable donations
under false pretences, unlawful gamblers and suspect lodgers in alehouses or
barns were all included in new legislation.

The 1824 Vagrancy Act served to rationalise the criminal law in relation
to vagrancy, replacing 27 previous statutes. This Act retained the well-
established threefold categorisation of offenders, but reduced the levels of
punishment: for the 'idle and disorderly' (beggars within their own parish)
punishment remained at one month's imprisonment; for 'rogues and
vagabonds' (beggars outside their own parish) imprisonment was reduced
from six to three months; and 'incorrigible' (recidivist) rogues were liable to
one rather than two years imprisonment. The passing of convicted vagrants
from parish to parish was also abolished (Rose, 1988). The latter provision
was in large part a response to the spiralling costs of passing large numbers
of vagrants, rather than reflecting any impetus towards the decriminalisation
of vagrancy.

In the years following the 1824 Act, there was a rapid increase in the
rates of imprisonment of vagrants, not necessarily because of new and
harsher attitudes, but rather as a consequence of the increasing levels of
unemployment during this period of economic depression. The numbers of
imprisoned paupers increased from 7,092 in 1825 to 15,624 in 1832, but
nevertheless the legislation was becoming virtually unenforceable in some
areas of the country due to the sheer weight of numbers. This was the case in
Liverpool, for example, at the height of Irish migration to this port city
(Rose, 1988). Privy searches of lodging houses continued, but there was no
longer any pretence of reforming vagrants by means of confining them in
houses of correction.

The 1824 Act, like many of its forerunners, was a catch-all piece of legislation directed at miscellaneous forms of deviance: at 'riotous and indecent' prostitute women as well as at beggars and vagrants. It was also an early form of 'sus' law in its inclusion of anyone deemed to be leading a potentially suspicious lifestyle: those sleeping rough as well as those begging or wandering abroad. For these groups, the conventions of common law were overturned, in that the legal system now presumed their guilt rather than their innocence.

The New Poor Law was passed in 1834 and established two important principles: the 'workhouse test' and the principle of 'less eligibility'. The workhouse test, prefigured by legislation passed a century earlier, confirmed the trend towards confining and spatially controlling the poor by means of offering only indoor relief, and thus requiring the desperate poor to leave whatever homes they might have in order to receive aid. The less eligibility principle determined that relief should be at a level below that earned by the poorest labourer, but even this was not enough to assuage the fears of the Victorian bourgeoisie, and the explicitly deterrent casual wards system was introduced in mid-century. Worse even than the conditions in the workhouses, the casual wards offered the barest comfort and minimal shelter to those who elected, or were forced into, the transient life (Golden, 1992).

A period of transition

The first three decades of the twentieth century represented a period of transition in the history of the regulation of vagrancy. At the beginning of this period, prosecutions and convictions remained at a high level, dropping sharply by the mid-1930s when there developed a certain level of public sympathy for vagrants, culminating in the limited decriminalisation of vagrancy under the 1935 Act. By the late-1930s, however, prosecutions for begging had once again reached a high level of over 3,500 per year (Rose, 1988).

In the interwar years, the police tended to leave rough sleepers alone, as long as they were in recognised places such as London's Embankment or under Charing Cross bridge, although periodic sweeps of the Embankment were conducted at times when there was a feeling that the numbers of vagrants residing there were becoming 'too high'. In 1933 John Parker, a convicted vagrant, died in suspicious circumstances in Winson Green prison. This event and the subsequent verdict of accidental death led to a public outcry and a call for an end to police harassment of rough sleepers under existing vagrancy legislation. Under the 1935 Vagrancy Act various conditions were set out that qualified the definition of someone as a 'rogue and a vagabond' as described in the 1824 Vagrancy Act. In particular, sleeping-out was no longer to be an offence in and of itself, but only if a person persisted in wandering about, failed to go to a reasonable place of shelter when so directed by a police officer, or posed a danger to public health (Rose, 1988). Immediately following this Act, convictions for vagrancy fell to a low of 335 in 1936, in contrast to around 15,000 per annum a century earlier.

The National Assistance Act of 1948 ended the Poor Law years and heralded the advent of the welfare state. Criminal law was replaced with civil legislation as a response to poverty, and in particular local authorities and the National Assistance Board were required to resettle vagrants and to rehouse those temporarily homeless (under section 21 (1) (b) of the Act). This provision signalled a shift in discourse towards regarding homelessness as a social problem in its own right rather than as symptomatic of the twin evils of idleness and fecklessness (Robson and Poustie, 1996). However, homelessness was not yet understood as evidence of poverty and housing need, but was defined either as a welfare problem or as evidence of individual pathology. In this sense the beliefs and assumptions of the Poor Law lived on into the brave new world of the welfare state. The Poor Law lived on in a physical sense too, with many former workhouses being turned into hostels and lodging-houses for the postwar homeless population.

(Re)discovering homelessness

The national conscience was awakened to the question of homelessness as never before during the 1960s. Academic and policy reports, the establishment of voluntary organisations such as Shelter and the Simon Community, official enquiries and a series of 'social problem' documentaries all served to propel the homeless to the forefront of the political and social agenda. In sharp contrast to the earlier postwar media and literary representations that had focused on the classic image of the tramp as being male, middle-aged and alcoholic, concern in this decade focused on women, families and young people: the new homeless. Although vagrancy legisaltion has persisted into the latter half of the twentieth century, by 1968 there were fewer than 500 prosecutions for begging, although this was soon to rise again to an average of 900-1300 prosecutions per annum in the early 1970s. Prosecutions for sleeping rough were also at a low level during this period (Rose, 1988).

During the late 1960s-early 1970s a number of reports were influential on the development of official discourses of homelessness, with for the first time homelessness being conceived of as primarily a housing problem, rather than as evidence of pathology or criminality (see for example the Greve Report, 1971 and the Morris Report, 1975). There was dissatisfaction with the inadequacies of the 1948 National Assistance Act and growing pressure for legislative reform: a particular concern was that housing rather than social work departments should take responsibility for the homeless (Robson and Poustie, 1996). At the same time the Brennan Committee (1971) sat to investigate the implementation of the 1824 Vagrancy Act and concluded that sleeping rough - and to a lesser extent begging - were social problems rather than criminal acts (Rose, 1988). However, and rather contradictorily, a 1974 Home Office report (Working Party on Vagrancy and Street Offences Working Paper) conflated vagrancy and street prostitution and, at least by implication, criminalised the former by virtue of its association with the latter. One hundred and fifty years earlier, the 1824

Vagrancy Act had dedicated itself to dealing both with vagrants and with 'riotous and indecent' prostitutes.

The 1977 Housing (Homeless Persons) Act satisfied in a limited way some of the demands for reform made during the previous decade, but it also maintained a connection with some of the earlier Poor Law traditions. In this sense, civil and criminal legislation on homelessness continued to operate in tandem into the latter quarter of the twentieth century. The 1977 Act did transfer responsibility for homelesseness from social services to housing departments, symbolising its recognition as a housing rather than welfare problem. It also extended local authority provision for the homeless, but disappointed many campaigners in its modification of the notion of rights to housing on the part of the homeless. Critics also detected echoes of the Old Poor Law in the 'local connection' amendment that attempted to spatially confine those in urgent housing need to their places of origin. Ancient fears of bogus claimants of support also informed the legislative distinction between the 'intentionally' and 'unintentionally' homeless, and comparisons with the earlier separation of the poor into categories of 'deserving' and 'undeserving' scarcely need to be drawn.

The fiscal and moral rectitude of the 1970s gave way in the early 1980s to a limited degree of sympathy for the homeless, as the visible numbers living on the streets grew to unprecedentedly high levels in modern times, including large numbers of the obviously vulnerable new homeless. By the late 1980s and early 1990s however, this limited degree of sympathy began to evaporate as the numbers of homeless people continued to increase, and the discourse shifted once more towards criminalisation. Interpretation of the 1977 Act narrowed progressively, at the same time as the adoption of short term solutions such as the Rough Sleepers' Initiative increased in popularity.

Prosecutions for begging and sleeping rough under the 1824 Act began to increase rapidly, rising from 573 convictions for begging in London in 1988, to 1,396 in 1989 (Kelly, 1990). In 1990, almost 1,500 British young people were prosecuted under this legislation for the 'offences' of begging and sleeping rough (Dibblin, 1991), and in 1994 the Criminal Justice and Public Order Act was passed, serving to criminalise the formerly civil offences of travelling and squatting. These modern responses to the premodern condition of homelessness have created quintessential status offences under what we might call the New Vagrancy Acts (Davis et al, 1994).

On the civil legislative front, the 1996 Housing Act served to encourage the provision of short-term accommodation for those without any form of shelter, for example under the Rough Sleepers' Initiative, but generally to reduce the availability of emergency accommodation for the homeless. Furthermore, the Act provided that those accepted as homeless by the local authorities would now be entitled only to temporary rather than permanent rehousing, thus breaking with the principle established almost twenty years previously under the 1977 Act.

The establishment of the Rough Sleepers' Initiative reflected the official discourse of homelessness: first, that it was primarily a metropolitan phenomenon, and second that rooflessness equals 'real' homelessness, and is therefore the only form of homelessness deserving of government-directed attempts to 'solve the problem' (Randall and Brown, 1993). The subsequent extension of the initiative to other towns and cities in England and Scotland has done little to alter the perception of homelessness as an urban and primarily metropolitan problem. At the time of writing, campaigners have lobbied unsuccessfully for its extension to Wales, and little if any central governmental attention has been directed towards rural areas anywhere in Britain (Shelter Cymru, 1998).

Rural vagrancy: the case of North Wales

Concentration on English (and to a lesser extent Scottish) homelessness is not confined to contemporary times: although the country as a whole, and the northern districts in particular are both economically and socially disadvantaged, the question of homelessness in largely rural Wales has been subject to consistent neglect. This neglect of the rural vagrant is all the more striking given that, historically, much vagrancy has in fact been a rural phenomenon, or has had its roots in rural poverty. Not surprisingly, therefore, the relatively little historical evidence that exists concerning crime and vagrancy in Wales is almost entirely confined to the southern industrial districts, areas which arguably have more in common with urban areas across the border than with the rural north of the country. There is little if any academic documentation of the treatment of North Walian vagrants, comparable to this account from the south:

> Mary Jones otherwise Gordon otherwise Murray being brought Before This Court, And it Appearing that she is a Notorious Vagrant having endeavoured to Impose on the Inhabitants of ye Town of Swansea by saying she was married to one William Jones, a wine cooper of the same Town, which Appears to be false. It is Ordered that the said Mary Jones be stripped from the wast upwards and publickly whipped upon Tuesday ye Eleventh day of April Instant between ye Hours of Ten and Twelve of the Clock in the forenoon of the same Day at ye s[ai]d Town of Cowbridge from ye East to the west Gate of ye s[ai]d Town (Grant, 1988:33).

The following brief excursion into the history of vagrancy in North Wales is based on occasional scattered references within the historical literature, and on local archival materials, including quarter session rolls, statements from workhouse masters, and local oral histories. Isolated accounts in the literature refer to the practice of begging in Anglesey as once being a commonplace activity. In the late 14th and early 15th centuries, it was the custom of the newly-married to beg their way through the first year of marriage. The male partner went off in search of work that was dependent upon harvesting cycles, whilst the female partnered an older women in order to participate in begging for cheese, wool, hemp and flax; these female partnerships were known locally as *gwragedd cawsa* (Beier, 1985).

At around the same time, the devastating effect of rural poverty led to a massive level of out-migration of men from the neighbouring county of Caernarfonshire, which contributed in turn to a situation where three-quarters of all households were headed by single women. Female paupers in the county outnumbered males by as much as ten to one, and thus we can deduce (although the documentary evidence is rather slight) that women predominated also among the vagrant and itinerant populations of this corner of north-west Wales.

Anglesey has been described as being almost 'perfectly agrarian' during the 18th and early-19th centuries (Ellis, 1987), although by the second half of the 19th century the demand for skilled farm labour began to diminish, at a time when agricultural modernisation led to the establishment of larger and less labour-intensive farms. Farm workers were no longer required all year round, and work became predominantly seasonal in order to meet the fluctuating demands of farm work such as draining and ditching. Agricultural workers were also being subject to radical changes in housing tenure and land use, at a time of widespread evictions from tied properties and the enclosure of common land.

The Anglesey quarter session rolls for the period 1860-1869 list 176 summary convictions for the offence of 'begging, vagrancy and desertion of family' out of a total of 1,500 offences listed. A large number of these convictions originated from particular areas of Anglesey such as the more affluent town of Beaumaris, as well as the rural parishes of Brynsiencyn and Llanerchymedd. However, most of these convicted beggars were not of local origin: out of 24 convictions for begging in 1862, 20 of those listed had names indicating non-Welsh origins. This points to a transient population of immigrant tramps and vagrants, a feature of island life heavily influenced by the port town of Holyhead with its ferry crossings to and from Ireland. This transient population was also reported to be involved in other crimes such as petty theft: for example, the Anglesey quarter sessions for 1867 reported the cases of two English-speaking tramps who had stolen clothing from an empty cottage, and another case of a huckster pretending to wrap three halfcrowns in a piece of paper and sell them for one shilling (Ellis, 1987). Victorian fears of the supposed criminality of the Irish migrant undoubtedly helped to draw this population to the attention of the criminal justice system.

The second half of the 19th century saw a high proportion of crimes listed under the vagrancy acts: in 1848, for example, just under 2,000 summary convictions were recorded for the whole of Wales, with 40% (877 cases) being listed under the vagrancy legislation. In North Wales, the Tywyn, Barmouth and Corwen occurrence books for 1884-99 reported that 26% of 723 recorded crimes were charged under the vagrancy acts. The recorded overall increase in crime during this period may partly be accounted for by the willingness of the North Wales police to record the formerly largely ignored crimes of vandalism and minor disorder among isolated rural communities (North Wales police, 1998).

However, this 'rising tide of crime' can also be linked to the increased mobility of the population, and in particular to the thousands of migrants passing through North Wales, with undoubtedly many vagrants to be counted among their number. This was a period that witnessed the building of the Ffestiniog to Porthmadog railway line in the south of the region, as well as the primary coastal rail route between Holyhead in the west of Anglesey to Chester just across the English border. This major work drew in thousands of labourers to the area, with accompanying high levels of drunkenness and disorder:

> On one occasion the authorities had to stand idly by while hundreds of English and Irish navvies fought a pitched battle lasting three days during the construction of the Chester to Holyhead line ... [This marked a] ... steadily deteriorating situation in the social fabric - near destitution with its attendant evils of pauperism and alcoholism [which was] widely prevalent, and a generally embittered workforce largely devoid of hope and becoming increasingly cynical in its attitude towards authority (North Wales police, 1998:1).

The supposed 'crisis' of the nineteenth century 'criminal vagrant' needs to be located within the context of wider social, economic and political changes that were taking place during this period. Industrialisation and urbanisation meant that the once dominant agricultural lifestyle no longer exerted the same control functions in relation to the rural working classes, who were migrating in large numbers to the towns and the cities (O'Connor, 1963). The Irish famine of 1845-9 brought large numbers of migrants into both the north and south of Wales via sea ports such as Holyhead and Newport (Jones, 1977).

The criminal vagrant was constructed as representing the antithesis of Welsh community and cultural values, with this 'dead loss to the community' being held responsible for 'chartist and industrial unrest, rural incendiarism, increases in petty crime and a general lowering of urban standards of health, behaviour and morality' (Jones, 1977:313). In particular, these vagrant 'outsiders' were accorded three main characteristics: their dirty clothing and habits; their visible destitution and illness; and their 'evil disposition'. In this way, Welsh vagabonds became criminalised and deemed unworthy of poor relief:

> vagrants, as a class, deserve but little pity, and ought rather to be under the cognisance of the police than the poor law officer. They are, for the most part, if not criminals, at least, on the verge of crime (Master of the Wrexham workhouse, 1848; in Jones, 1977:314).

Crime became conflated with disorder, and simple criminal acts began to symbolise the widespread social and economic malaise that was sweeping the country's lower classes. Dominant discourses of class were compounded by newly-emerging and pseudo-scientific notions of the 'criminal type', identifiable by an individual's association with a 'mobile criminal fraternity' and membership of a 'hereditary criminal class' (Jones, 1992). This interpretation of the dangerous criminal was conveniently constructed at a time when vagrants, released convicts and prostitutes were causing concern for the authorities. In North Wales, vagrants were being charged with malicious and criminal acts such as arson, although there is evidence to suggest that such criminality was in some cases provoked by the refusal of poor relief in certain counties. One presiding judge remarked on a particular case in 1868 that the vagrants 'were in some sort of way driven to this', yet such expressions of sympathy did not affect the severity of sentences, which ranged from four to eight years of penal servitude (Jones, 1977).

The vagrant thus became an ideal type, a scapegoat who could be blamed for an actual or perceived rise in crime and disorder. Furthermore, this criminalisation of the vagrant provided the justification for enforcing local mechanisms of social control:

> For the future every tramp met by officers must be thoroughly searched. The lodging houses visited and their bundles turned over. Then I feel confident nearly every tramp will stop coming into the country and we shall be almost free of crime (Order of the Chief Constable of Radnorshire, 1885; in Jones, 1977:312).

In Bangor, a workhouse committee recommended that the following system be set up in order to control vagrancy in the locality:

> Each vagrant on the morning following the day of his admission is after breakfast to be taken to the stone-breaking cell and has to break 3 cwt of stones and to throw the same out through the iron grating and then to be discharged if admitted by a white ticket. If admitted by a blue ticket he is to be taken to another cell and is to perform the same task and then to the third cell and is not to be discharged till 9 o'clock in the morning of the second day after admission, and if admitted by a red ticket he has to perform the same task as the one with the blue ticket and that for three days and is to be discharged at 9 o'clock on the fourth day after admission. A white ticket is to be supplied on the first visit, a blue ticket on the second or subsequent visit and a red ticket if two visits are made within a month (Workhouse Committee, Friday 29 November, 1895).

There was no single vagrant type at this time, but rather they were understood as belonging to many different categories: 'the professional English tramps, young urban outcasts, young rural escapees, temporarily destitute mechanics, artisans and agricultural labourers, "immoral" females, girls escaping from masters and factory work, and the Irish' (W. D. Boase, 1848; in Jones, 1977:317). However, the classic stereotype remained that of the 'professional tramp' or 'gentleman of the road', the vagrant who, it was believed, took to the road in order to avoid regular work. For many reasons discussed in more detail in chapter three, the romantic yet feared figure of the tramp came to dominate the public imagination and to become almost synonymous with the condition of vagrancy. These tramps travelled the countryside in small groups, sometimes working here and there, but more often begging from house to house or openly in the street. They were easily recognised by their 'dirty appearance, long coats, deep pockets, walking sticks and pipes' (ibid:319).

By definition a highly mobile person, the tramp established a good network of communications, and developed mental maps of the best places to stay and gain alms. There is evidence that 'cadger's maps' existed, inscribed with a legend intelligible only to others 'on the tramp', and indicating places where bread might be obtained and warning of others where the supplicant would be likely to meet with moral stricture or worse (Rose, 1988). Another frequent method of communication were the messages written on workhouse walls, to be read by fellow tramps:

> Notice to our pals - Bristol Jack and Burslem was here on the 15th of April, bound for Montgomeryshire for the summer season. Wrexham is head-quarters now. [And] George Day and William Jackson, 7th November 1865, bound for Portmadoc (Jones, 1977:319).

Into the twentieth century, the notion of the vagrant as tramp became increasingly well-established throughout British culture. The tramp was the subject of popular songs and literature, a cultural legacy that tended to support the commonplace notion that the tramp was confined to urban England and lowland Scotland (Burn, 1855; Rose, 1988). Vagrancy in more isolated and rural areas has been less well-documented, and so the following oral historical accounts are valuable in providing accounts of the social position of the tramp in rural North Wales:

> In the 1920s, after the First World War, there was very large numbers of 'Gentlemen of the road' better known as tramps. As we have two large hay barns in the kennels, we also had our share of tramps sleeping for the night in the hay barn. Huw-Mul-Bach was one who often slept in the hay barn. One morning about 7 am Huw knocked on our back door and my mother opened it. She saw Huw standing there with his cap in his hand, filled with about 12 eggs. He'd found where the old hen was laying in the hay barn, he'd put the eggs in his cap and handed them to my mother. This act of honesty impressed my mother very much. She made Huw some tea and some bread and cheese (Tim Davies, early 1980s, Llangefni archives).

> 'Do you remember if there were many tramps in those days?' Tramps? You're telling me! My old home was on the roadside between Machynlleth and Llanidloes. A tramp would never pass our house. They were never refused you know. They'd have an old tin with tea in the bottom and they'd ask for hot water and my Mother would ask if they'd got something to eat with it and they'd say no, and she'd cut them some bread and butter and a big lump of cheese. 'Oh! God bless you!' they'd say ... The same ones would come periodically. They knew where to go you see. I remember one coming one night and he wanted to sleep in the hay barn, hay loft. So my Father told him, Now look, he said there's no matches going there. I'm going to empty your pockets before you go. He puts his matches and his tobacco and his money and whatever else he has on the table and they were there for him when he got up in the morning, and my Father had given him some extra money. He used to come periodically to sleep in the hay loft, but he'd never let them take matches. On the condition he emptied his pockets (Mrs Thomas, early 1980s, Llangefni archives).

However, such sympathetic accounts did not mean that in the early twentieth century vagrancy was no longer constructed as a social problem. The often romantic notion of the 'professional tramp' as an unkempt but essentially honest individual served in part to obscure the true extent of homelessness, in that - although they were only ever a small minority - tramps came to represent 'true' homelessness within the popular imagination. Furthermore, while there may have been a degree of tolerance for a few characters perceived as rugged individualists, at the same time there was a continued criminalisation of the vagrant life. Arguably, such sentimental notions are most in evidence when levels of homelessness are particularly high. Sympathetic treatment of the vagrant, at least by the public if not by the Poor Law authorities, may be in evidence at times of economic depression, but the social position of the tramp (and other homeless figures) has always been tenuous at best. A romantic idealisation of the freedoms of the tramping life can all too quickly transmute into demonisation of the criminal vagrant. Literary and auto/biographical representations of vagrancy and homelessness are explored in detail in the following chapter.

3 Representing homelessness and crime

> The body of statute can be seen as a sustained and elaborate commentary on human activity, which is of necessity categorical, explicit, univocal. The press, on the other hand, provides a body of commentary which can be multi-vocal, inexplicit, suggestive and ambiguous, exploiting the possibilities of human absurdity and the inability to be exactly precise. And we must remember that both the press and the law, of course, can be equally misleading and unreliable guides to the actual behaviour of contemporary people (Bell, 1991:19).

Chapter two traced the history of legislative responses to the vagrant and the tramp. The categorical nature of statute notwithstanding, there was often a gap between legal discourse and actual treatment of homeless people. The harsh punishments decreed for vagrancy in the later medieval period, for example, were often not put into practice. Conversely, the social welfare rhetoric of the late 20th century has served at times to mask a punitive approach to the embarrassing spectacle of homelessness, an unwanted reminder of poverty amidst affluence.

The vagrant, the rogue and the vagabond - categories constructed over some seven centuries of legal discourse - are also characters who appear (and disappear and reappear) within our literary and cultural traditions. Whether we take legislation and literature to be equally misleading - or equally accurate - 'guides to the actual behaviour of contemporary people', arguably both serve to provide clues to the nature of popular fears, hopes and preoccupations in relation to the question of homelessness and crime.

The task of analysing the literature of homelessness and crime has fallen mainly to historians and literary critics rather than to criminologists (Denning, 1986; Rose, 1988; Kinney, 1990. See Beresford, 1979, for a sociological account). There have been few or no attempts to review this literature as a whole, with commentators preferring to concentrate on specific historical periods (Bell, 1991; Sargado, 1977), or on particular authors (Loughrey and Treadwell, 1986). This literature is extensive and diverse, and any review must therefore be highly selective. However, the adoption of a broad perspective helps to reveal the recurrent themes and characters, the contradictions and commonalities of this rich tradition.

For reasons of concision and coherence, only British sources have been considered, but the importance of early individual works such as Martin Luther's *Liber Vagatorum*, as well as the influence of the Spanish and French picaresque literary traditions should be acknowledged. Exemplars are drawn from a wide range of sources: rogue pamphlets, canting dictionaries, plays and songs, autobiographies, Christian tracts, docudramas and novels. Highly varied in terms of literary merit and popular appeal, these works are by turn tragic, comic, satirical and romantic.

Elizabethan rogue pamphlets

The vitality and exuberance of Elizabethan life is nowhere better seen and enjoyed than in the rogue books and cony-catching pamphlets of the sixteenth and early seventeenth centuries. And what a colorful and witty crowd of ragamuffins and renegades these Elizabethan rogues and vagabonds are; cutpurses, hookers, palliards, dummerers, jarkmen, doxies and crosbiters; counterfeit cranks, abraham men, bawdy-baskets, walking morts, kinchin cos, and priggers of prancers; minstrels, gypsies, peddlers, tinkers, jugglers and bearwards.

Yet

On the highway too ... Disturbers of the peace, enemies of law and order, the terror of the simple farmer, the most pressing problem of the Tudor years of England, these throngs of beggars and their wenches were never absent from city or shire (Kinney, 1990: 11-12).

Kinney thus both documents and subscribes to long-established notions of a romantic yet threatening vagrant underworld, as developed within the picaresque and subsequent literary traditions. He along with most commentators, historical and contemporary, is enchanted with and fascinated by the vivid diversity of the Tudor and Elizabethan underworld (see Aydelotte 1913; Judges 1930). In this section, and in the following section on the canting language of rogues and vagabonds, there will be an exploration of the rogue pamphlets and pamphleteers of the late 16th and early 17th centuries. Writers such as Harman (1566) and Dekker (1608;1612) have been variously described as proto-novelists and as hack writers; they were journalists and magistrates, chroniclers and even, some claim, early sociologists (Kinney, 1990; Sargado,1977). They were certainly highly influential writers, at once providing popular entertainment, a chronicle of social life, and a classification of the then amorphous mass of vagrants, beggars and petty criminals. In short the penny pamphlets combined 'the qualities of romantic fiction and close observation' (Judges, 1930: xiii).

Commentators vary as to the degree of historical accuracy they attribute to the rogue pamphlets, which themselves claimed to be true representations of social life and which for centuries afterwards continued to be widely cited as authoritative sources. Undoubtedly there was much exaggeration, but equally some of the cases cited by Harman (1566), in his *Caveat for*

Common Cursitors Vulgarly Called Vagabonds (later simply *Caveat*), have been matched with official records, their offences and punishments being listed along with the class of vagabond to which they belonged (Aydelotte, 1913). Some of Harman's rogues were uncovered in the privy searches of 1571-2, while others are mentioned in the Middlesex quarter session rolls in the period up until 1590 (Aydelotte, 1913; Kinney,1990). Perhaps a more important point is that these tracts were widely believed at the time to be accurate: appearing at a time when the popular press was becoming well-established, they can be understood as an early form of crime news, documenting the social and political concerns of their day (Kinney,1990).

The rogue pamphlets were the first extensive crime media, and in terms of style they can be placed somewhere between today's tabloid press and the true crime genre. The pamphlets also worked as proto-novels, and we shall see later the ways in which the characters of these penny pamphlets reappear in various guises in the popular literature of succeeding centuries. They were also reforming tracts intended to deter begging and vagrancy and to encourage punishment of these offences. Harman was a magistrate and combined his writing with a mission to expose vagabonds as fakes, often acting in a more or less private capacity in his punishment of rogues and vagabonds. He was known to remove beggars' licences from rogues; to attempt to prove false the claims of 'counterfeit cranks' and 'dummerers'; and to subject such people to summary justice rather than consigning them to a court of law.

In this very practical sense, the rogue literature and the criminal justice process were intertwined, but the influence of the Elizabethan penny pamphlets extended also to the formulation of criminal law. It is also surely not accidental that the rogue pamphlets were most popular during this period of transition from medieval Christian notions of poverty and vagrancy, to the criminalisation of these same conditions under the influence of emergent mercantile capitalism.

The pamphleteers clearly did not invent new categories of rogues and vagabonds but, drawing on emerging popular and legal opinion, did serve to codify and classify these formerly rather amorphous categories. Thomas Dekker (1608;1612), a popular hack writer who borrowed extensively from other works, compared his sophisticated classification of 26 types of beggar and vagabond with the simple grouping of vagabonds, faitors, robardsmen, draw-latches and sturdy beggars recognised during the medieval period (Kinney,1990). As late as 1550 the legal classification of vagrancy had been relatively simple, with distinctions being drawn between the 'sick and impotent' and the 'sturdy vagabond' (Petition to Privy Council, 1552; Judges, 1930).

Twenty years later, the vague category of vagabond was given more precise definition and it is impossible to think that Harman's *Caveat* of 1566 was not a major influence here. In 1572 it was declared that:

> Proctors ... and all other ydle persones goinge about in the Countrye of the said Realme, using subtyll craftye or unlawful Games or Playes, and some of them fayninge themselves to have knowledge in Phisnomye [physiognomy] Palmestrye or other abused Scyences ... And all and

51

everye persone and persones whole and mightye in Body and able to labour ... and all Fencers and Bearwardes Comon Players in Enterludes [ie unlicensed actors in travelling plays] and Minstrels ... all Juglers Pedlars Tynkers and Petye Chapmen, shall wander abroade, and have not Lycense of two Justices of the Peace ... shalbee taken adjudged and deemed Roges Vacaboundes and Sturdy Beggars ... (14 Elizabeth c.5. s.5; in Kinney, 1990:13).

The works of Thomas Harman and Thomas Dekker merit closer examination, with each representating a particular period and style within the picaresque literature. The rogue pamphlets, of which there are some twenty to twenty five, may be divided into an early period (1552-1592) which includes authors such as Awdeley (1561) and Harman (1566), and a later period (1592-1616) which is characterised by work from journalists such as Dekker (1608;1612) and Rid (1612). While the apparent honesty and simplicity of the earlier works have been contrasted unfavourably with the unscrupulous plagiarism and harsher satire of the later hack writers by commentators such as Aydelotte (1913), it would perhaps be fairer to say that in both cases 'we really turn away from fact and toward fiction; real crime and anguish are eventually buried in story, joke, legend, and mythopoeic history' (Kinney,1990:55).

Thomas Harman: A Caveat for Common Cursitors Vulgarly Called Vagabonds

This is indeed a work expressed in a simple style, yet it combines close social observation with entertaining fictional or semi-fictional accounts of picaresque adventures. The vagabond is simultaneously condemned and romanticised, represented as both criminal and anti-hero. This proved to be a successful formula in Harman's own times, with his work being reprinted several times and widely imitated by his contemporaries. Indeed, and as we shall see later, such portrayals of the 'seductions and repulsions' of crime have proven to be a perenially popular literary device (Katz, 1988). Deriving from the three main classes of upright men, rogues and palliards, Harman provides us with 24 categories of rogues and vagabonds, painting for us in colourful language stories of rufflers, upright men, hookers, rogues and wild rogues, priggers of prancers, palliards, fraters and patricos, abraham men, whipjacks, counterfeit cranks, dummerers, drunken tinkers, peddlers, jarkmen, demanders for glimmer, bawdy-baskets, autem-morts and walking morts, doxies and dells, kinchin morts and kinchin cos.

The ruffler, often a former soldier, headed the beggars' hierarchy, but after a year or so on the road his social status declined and he became known as an upright man - 'the second insect of this unseemly sort' (Harman, 1566; in Judges, 1930:69). The upright man steals or demands money rather than begs, has droit de seigneur over vagrant women, and initiates others into the subculture of vagabondage. Harman presents the reader with elements of both social documentary and literary narrative, and in this way the amorphous medieval understanding of vagrancy came to be defined as a distinct criminal underworld with its strict hierarchy and initiation ceremonies, populated by characters such as the rufflers and the upright men who were to be feared for their semi-criminality and sexual licentiousness.

A rogue was not as strong as an upright man, but rather made a pretence of weakness or illness in order to seek alms. Rogues were primarily frauds, often carrying false licences and passes from justices of the peace. In contrast, 'a wild rogue is he that is born a rogue. He is more subtle and more given by nature to all kind of knavery than the other, as beastly begotten in barns and bushes, and from his infancy traded up in treachery' (ibid:78). While condemning both characters, Harman believed that the born beggar or wild rogue was less culpable as he had little choice over his vocation.

Harman reserved greatest vitriol for the third general class, the palliards or clapperdudgeons. Palliards faked serious injury by means of plants such as spearwort and ratsbane, and they travelled wearing patched cloaks and carrying faked licences. Harman believed that the class of palliard was found most often in the Celtic nations:

> There be many Irishmen that go about with counterfeit licences. And if they perceive you will straitly examine them, they will immediately say they can speak no English ... The most of these that walk about be Welshmen (ibid:80-1).

Harman was one of the last social chroniclers to construct the Welsh rather than the Irish as the most feared folk devils, a situation soon to change with increasing levels of Irish migration to Britain.

For the most part, the female classes of rogues and vagabonds are described in terms of their sexuality. Harman, for example, indulges his love of alliteration in his description of the bawdy-baskets who: 'trade their lives in lewd, loathsome lechery. Amongst them all is but one honest woman, and she is of good years' (Harman, 1566; in Kinney 1990:137). Harman describes the demanders for glimmer and bawdy-baskets as women engaged in promiscuity or prostitution, doxies as promiscuous companions to upright men, and dells as young women with as yet no sexual experience. Such inexperience was not equated with innocence, however, for he describes such young women born into vagrancy as: 'these wild Dells, being traded up with their monstrous mothers, must of necessity be as evil or worse, than their parents ... but such buds, such blossoms, such evil seed sown, will [be] worse being grown' (ibid:144).

Marriage or widowhood did not exempt the vagrant woman from being considered sexually licentious: a minority were considered to be legally married women (autem-morts), and many more to have feigned widowhood (walking-morts), but neither were considered to be respectable in nature. Walking morts lived by 'begging, bitchery [prostitution] or bribery', and of the autem-morts, Harman says:

> And they be as chaste as a cow I have, that goeth to bull every moon, with what bull she careth not (Harman,1566; in Judges 1930:99-100).

Once again, Harman established a trend that has persisted into contemporary times: that of labelling the vagrant woman as sexually deviant.

Thomas Dekker: O Per Se O

Dekker (1608; 1612) is understood to have been a plagiarist and a hack-writer, and his work is largely derivative of Harman's *Caveat*. However he does add some new categories of rogues and vagabonds, reflecting the social concerns and preoccupations of his time. For Harman the abraham men were those who faked lunacy in order to beg alms, while Dekker describes such characters as moon-men or mad-men. Indeed, Dekker conflates lunacy (pretended or otherwise) with other forms of deviance, variously describing moon-men as fortune-telling and poaching gypsies and as 'Tawny Moor's bastards' and 'Red-ochre-men'. Their racial minority status, like their lunacy, is alleged to be false, and these 'counterfeit Egyptians' are compared disfavourably with the 'true English beggar' (Dekker, 1608; in Kinney 1990:243).

Within half a century, Harman's general disparagement of Welsh and Irish beggars had hardened into Dekker's more complex racial discourse. Disparate groups such as lunatics and gypsies, the Irish and North Africans were conflated into one frightening spectacle of deviance and disorder. The figure of the gypsy (whether real or counterfeit) emerged as a particularly feared folk devil, as did the Irish who were by now understood as a separate class of vagabond. Dekker's world-view was a more bleak one than Harman's and was relatively unrelieved by humour or sympathy for the vagrant. His was a heavily religious imagery, one that perceived human life as corrupt and depraved, with only a fragile Christian candlelight to illuminate a darkened world: thus *Lantern and Candlelight* (1608) was set in Hell, with vagrants depicted as devil-worshippers (Beier, 1985)

O Per Se O (1612) was simply a revised and expanded version of *Lantern and Candlelight*, taking its title from the refrain of a contemporary beggars' song. *O Per Se O* begins with a canting dictionary copied largely from Harman, and is followed by extensive descriptions of cony-catchers, frauds, cozeners and tricksters. Dekker claims to have gained his knowledge of vagrancy first hand from 'my devilish schoolmaster', the eponymous anti-hero O Per Se O, but this claim is likely to have been false as his work is so clearly plagiarised from Harman and other sources. Indeed, elsewhere Dekker reflects on the deceptions commonly practised by his own profession (Aydelotte, 1913). There is thus little that is new in Dekker's work, but the interest for us lies not in his originality but in his reflection of contemporary concerns. In particular Dekker, far more than Harman, was concerned with dangerous places as well as dangerous people. Dekker was preoccupied with the bousing and stalling kens - the alehouses and houses that received stolen goods. While these appeared in Harman as incidental locations, for Dekker 'these houses are the nurseries of rogues and thieves' (ibid:367).

The fear of dangerous places extended to the commonplace fairs and festivals, of which some one thousand were held annually: prohibitions on these fairs were frequently imposed but were seldom effective. Chroniclers of the period held that vagrants sought to establish themselves at these festivals as 'lords of the fair', and even that there was an annual beggars' fair at Tewkesbury, although these are contested claims (Beier, 1985). Nevertheless, vivid contemporary descriptions such as Dekker's account of the Tewkesbury fair were instrumental in constructing them as symbolic locations:

> you shall see more rogues than ever were whipped at the cart's arse, and more beggars than ever came dropping out of Ireland. If you look upon them, you would think you lived in Henry the Sixth's time, and that Jack Cade and his rebellious ragamuffins were there mustering ... The buyers and sellers are both alike, tawny sun-burned rascals, and they flock in such troops, that it shows as if Hell were broke loose. The shopkeepers are thieves, and the chapmen rogues, beggars and whores; so that to bring a purse-full of money hither were madness, for it is sure to be cut (Dekker, 1612; in Judges 1930:368-9).

The connection between this description of the beggars' fair and contemporary moral panics concerning new age travellers and their festivals scarcely needs to be made.

The canting dictionaries

> Here I set before the good reader the lewd, lousy language of these loitering lusks and lazy lorels ... which language they term pedlars French, an unknown tongue only but to these bold, beastly, bawdy beggars and vain vagabonds, being half mingled with English when it is familiarly talked (Harman, 1566; in Judges, 1930:114).

The rogue pamphleteers regularly compiled canting dictionaries, with some three hundred words and phrases being recorded in Harman's literature of roguery. The documentation of beggars' cant was central to the aims of the rogue literature: it amused and entertained the reader of picaresque adventures; it helped to establish the vagrant life as a separate and exotic underworld or subculture; and it supported the scholarly pretensions of the pamphleteers.

Dekker, not surprisingly given his extensive plagiarism of the *Caveat*, echoes Harman's claim that canting originated in the 1530s, but unlike Harman who finds this tongue entertaining, Dekker makes an analogy between cant and the discord and conflict of the Biblical Tower of Babel. However, the origins of cant are almost certainly earlier than claimed by Harman and Dekker, at least in continental Europe where over two hundred words were listed in Martin Luther's *Liber Vagatorum* as early as the 1490s (Hotten and Thomas, 1932). The origins of the word itself are uncertain, probably deriving from the Latin *cantare* (to sing), although some believe it to be of Celtic origin (Beier, 1985). The language itself is a highly mixed one, drawing on Irish, Welsh, Scots and Cornish, as well as elements of Romany. Itinerant monks and returned soldiers made further contributions of Latinisms and words culled from various foreign campaigns (Kinney, 1990). Linguistically, 'cant' works at two levels: as a noun to describe the specialised language of vagabonds, and as the verb 'to beg' (Sargado, 1977).

Cant functioned as a means by which the various vagrant groups could establish a common lingua franca, thus facilitating internal communication and reducing the risk of detection when engaged upon frauds and misdemeanours. Paradoxically, this usage of specialised language allowed the authorities to identify the vagabond, and confessions to the use of cant were used in many criminal trials to define deviant status (Beier, 1985). The use of cant was undoubtedly widespread among vagrants, but the rogue literature tended to exaggerate its significance as a marker of a distinct and separate subculture, in that cant terms were also widespread among the general populace. However, the appeal of such vivid language to the chroniclers of rogue life was irresistible, and a lexicographical tradition was quickly established. Dekker, for example, asserted that not only was canting unique to vagabonds, but that such use of language was essential to the vagrant way of life. He describes, or imagines, an initiation ceremony thus:

> I, - do stall thee, - to the rogue, by virtue of this sovereign English liquor, so that henceforth it shall be lawful for you to cant ... to be a vagabond, and to speak that pedlar's French ... which is to be found among none but beggars (Dekker, 1608; in Judges, 1930:308).

Harman was the first systematically to document this 'peevish speech', and in this as in much else he has been widely imitated, although few have matched his love of alliteration. He gives us around 120 words, most of which refer to aspects of everyday life such as eating, drinking, money and accommodation. Fewer than twenty words relate directly to crime and the criminal justice process, but there are references to clying the jerk (being whipped), to chats (the gallows) and to queer-kens (prison-houses), all common features of the vagabond life. With little evidence of either irony or pride, the *Caveat* also includes references to Harman's own place within the canting tongue: the stocks became known as the harmans, while the parish constable was named the harman-beck.

Although canting dictionaries appeared in Greene (1591) and Rid (1610) as well as Dekker, these were all largely derivative of Harman. There was little significant further development until the 18th century, with the appearance of the anonymous *A New Canting Dictionary* in 1725, and Grose's *Classical Dictionary of the Vulgar Tongue* in 1785. The lexicons of this period were considerably more extensive, and the classifications more complex, than their 16th century counterparts. The *New Canting Dictionary*, for example, cited 'gypsy' as the 58th order of canter in contrast to Harman's 24 classes of vagabond, while Francis Grose listed thousands of words, in contrast to the three hundred or so compiled within the early rogue literature.

In many other respects, however, there was a continuation with the earlier tradition. Grose, like Harman, combined scholarly effort with entertainment, accurate documentation with apocryphal stories, and detached observation with moral condemnation. Indeed, in the third edition of his work Grose acknowledged his debt to Harman, stating that his own dictionary was based on the *Caveat* plus three other anonymous works: *Hell upon Earth* (1703), *The Scoundrel's Dictionary* (1754) and *The Canting Academy* (nd). Grose reflected at length on the etymology of 'cant' which he believed to derive from the Old Northern French cant or chant, to sing, and was used from the early 16th century onwards to denote the 'whining speech of beggars'. He held that cant words derived from many diverse European, Oriental and classical as well as indigenous languages, and that the 'secret language' thus formed came to be used by the 'criminal and vagabond classes' during the 17th and 18th centuries (Grose, 1796).

Grose did not confine himself to modern conventions of lexicography but was frequently digressive and discursive. One of his longest entries related to gypsies, within which he combined scholarly reference, anecdote, moral instruction and social observation. His contemporaries were much concerned with vagabonds masquerading as gypsies, and although there is little historical evidence to support these fears, their existence as a distinct criminal subculture was accepted as fact (Beier, 1985). Grose tells us that gypsies are:

> ... a set of vagrants who ... pretend that they derive their origin from the ancient Egyptians ... They artificially discolour their faces, and speak a kind of gibberish peculiar to themselves. They rove up and down the country in large companies, to the great terror of the farmers ... As they live, so they lie together promiscuously, and they know not how to claim a property, either in their goods or children ... They stroll up and down all summer time in droves, and dextrously pick pockets, while they are telling fortunes (Grose, 1796: 175-77).

There are clear echoes here of Dekker's entry on 'moon-men' and Grose, like Dekker before him, went on to describe the initiation rituals of the vagrant life. Whereas Dekker makes only brief reference to 'stalling the rogue', Grose provides a lengthy, though not necessarily accurate, documentary account of this initiation process. He reports that a new recruit is required to recite the following oath:

> I Crank Cuffin, do swear to be a true brother, and that I will in all things obey the commands of the great tawny prince ... I will not teach anyone to cant, nor will I disclose any of our mysteries to them. I will take my prince's part against all who oppose him ... I will not conceal aught I win out of libkins, or from the ruffmans, but will preserve it for the use of the company. Lastly, I will cleave to my doxy wap... (Grose, 1796: 176).

Here Grose comes closer to the art of storytelling than he does to the conventions of lexicography. In doing so he continues the tradition of promoting the notions of a shadowy and criminal underworld while characterising the players as colourful figures, thus ensuring his enduring popularity as both entertainer and scholar.

For a century and a half, the *Classical Dictionary of the Vulgar Tongue* remained the most comprehensive of the canting dictionaries, to be replaced only in the mid-20th century by Partridge's *Dictionary of the Underworld* (1950; 1995). A volume of over 800 pages, this monumental work presented tens of thousands of entries on the argot of vagrants and on the criminal underworld. Partridge's coverage was encyclopaedic, historically encompassing the 16th to mid-20th centuries, and making geographic reference to South Africa, New Zealand and Australia, as well as the major sources of Britain and North America. A philologist by training, Partridge was also something of a social scientist and he presents a work that is both scholarly and entertaining. His sources include Grose and the major rogue pamphleteers such as Awdeley, Dekker, Greene and Harman, as well as 20th century lexicographers. In his own words, Partridge thus presents us with the definitive work on cant, which he defined as 'the vocabularies of crooks, criminals, racketeers, beggars, tramps, convicts, the commercial underworld, the drug traffic, the white slave traffic, and spivs' (Partridge, 1995: cover page).

The compilation of canting dictionaries has persisted into the late twentieth century, with Lionel Rose, providing a 'trampoloquia', or glossary of tramp cant. Rose (1988) traces the changing meanings of cant words over time with for example the abraham man familiar in Tudor times as someone who fakes lunacy in order to beg, coming to mean a veteran tramp in the inter-war years of the twentieth century. The word cant itself mutated into the Victorian back-door cant, or begging talk at tradesman's entrances.

Rose's trampoloquia captures a vivid sense of the continued and creative evolution of tramp cant, in that some words alter their meaning over time, some are dropped from usage, while still others are invented in response to changing circumstances. Rose captures a sense of the ways in which Victorian and Edwardian vagrants classified themselves, using evocative terms such as land squatters, muggers, haystack queens and high flyers. There was often a sense of irony, for example in the humourously euphemistic description of tramps as milestone inspectors and sons of rest. Subjected to centuries of categorisation as rogues and vagabonds, vagrants used vivid language to develop their own system of classification. In Victorian times, flatty described an outsider, someone unable to understand cant; in the early 20th century a prater was the itinerant tramp 'parson'; and the slummer of the inter-war years was the bourgeois evangelist who was fond of visiting the homeless in hostels and lodging-houses.

Augustan satirical drama: *The Beggar's Opera*

Political satire entered into the rogue literary tradition in the eighteenth century, with the production of John Gay's *The Beggar's Opera* in 1728 and Henry Fielding's *Jonathan Wild* in 1754 (Chandler, 1907). *The Beggar's Opera* was to be the most performed piece of the 18th century, and the dramatist Gay became emblematic of the political and social concerns of his time (Loughrey and Treadwell, 1986). Adapted in 1928 as the *Threepenny Opera* by Bertolt Brecht and Kurt Weill, this story has been interpreted as a universal fable: while this may be true, the popularity of the play rested also on its particular and local meanings, especially its commentary on 18th century political life.

The Beggar's Opera works as a satire both of politicians and of the conventions of the new and hugely popular Italian operatic format. In the

Opera, English and Irish folk songs replace Italian arias, and while canting language itself is not used Gay does draw on a popular and irreverent gallows humour. Gay is sympathetic to the rogue, but his main focus is on political corruption: he maintains a satiric humour throughout the play, rather than imitating the romantic conventions of the earlier picaresque literature (Bell, 1991). Set in the rookeries of St. Giles, *The Beggar's Opera* evokes the atmosphere of this underworld of alehouses, gin palaces and prisons. The setting quite deliberately epitomises the fear of dangerous places endemic among the new middle-classes who were concerned to move as far away as possible from inner London (Loughrey and Treadwell, 1986).

The Beggar's Opera moves beyond the moral instruction and popular sentiment of the early rogue literature and captures something of the social and political tensions of the Augustan age. Poised between the disappearance of the old feudal order and the newly emerging social order based on mercantile capitalism, bourgeois morality and the law of contract, the *Opera* thus expresses a more complex, contradictory and incomplete world-view, and 'this is why it does not have a proper happy ending, why the hero is not really moral, why the unity is incomplete' (Denning, 1986: 46).

Gay may not have been the first, as some have suggested, to compare the behaviour of politicians with that of beggars and thieves, but he did establish such satire as a highly successful metaphor of crime (Denning, 1986; Bell, 1991). He established a now commonplace but then highly controversial connection between the conventions of high and low society:

> Through the whole piece you may observe such a similitude of Manners in high and low life, that it is difficult to determine whether (in the fashionable vices) the fine Gentlemen imitate the Gentlemen of the Road, or the Gentlemen of the Road the fine Gentlemen (Gay, 1728, II, 64).

Gay's message, again pioneering in its day, was that at least the denizens of the underworld are openly and honestly criminal, unlike the politicians of respectable society. Furthermore, bourgeois and aristocratic rogues are protected by the law while the poorer classes are routinely and severely punished. The gallows appear as a comic and satiric theme throughout the opera, but their presence was a very real threat to contemporary rogues and vagabonds. At the end of the play, the criminal anti-hero Macheath faces the gallows and laments to the tune of the Elizabethan love song *Greensleeves*:

> Since laws were made for every degree to curb vice in others, as well as me, I wonder we hadn't better company, Upon Tyburn tree! But gold from law can take out the sting; And if rich men like us were to swing, T'would thin the land, such numbers to string Upon Tyburn tree! (Gay, 1728, III, 13).

In Gay's work, the beggar thus becomes a dignified and often sympathetic - though realistic and not overly romanticised - character. He, and although there are strong female characters within the opera the main anti-hero is male, also becomes a subversive figure, one capable of both inverting society's norms and conventions, and of embodying the fears and often secret desires of respectable society.

From romance to philanthropy: the 19th and early 20th centuries

During a period when urbanisation and capitalist development produced ever more diverse forms of poverty and vagrancy, and when popular literature was being produced in forms more varied and accessible than ever before, the picaresque figure of this period became a complex and multivocal one. At least three distinct traditions may be distinguished within the literature: the romantic, the autobiographic and the philanthropic. They will be addressed separately here, although inevitably there is a considerable overlap between these three categories.

The romantic tradition, although clearly present among some of the rogue pamphleteers, came into its own in Victorian and Edwardian times. Popularised via broadsheets and music hall songs, audiences were able to transfer their hopes and longings to the romantic figure of the vagrant, the wanderer with his putative freedoms. A second major genre was that of the tramp authors, in vogue from mid-19th century to the pre-war years. Taking the long established trend for claiming first-hand knowledge of vagrancy to its logical extent, the tramp authors based their appeal on their autobiographical narratives. While some undoubtedly did go 'on the tramp', others, motivated perhaps by economic profit or evangelical zeal, claimed fraudulently to have done so. In style, much of this work is presented and can be read as fiction, but in some texts there can also be detected the seeds of an early ethnographic and social documentary tradition. At around the same time, a parallel genre was established by philanthropists who went undercover in their research of vagrant lifestyles, and some of this work, too, may be understood as an early form of sociological work, in the methodological tradition of covert participant observation. These works were presented either as factual accounts or as biographies, but they nevertheless share the narrative drama of fictional or semi-fictional literature.

The romantic tradition

> Such was the curious dichotomy of public attitudes to the tramp; at times he was the menacing wild man of the woods, at others the enviable personification of freedom (Rose, 1988:107).

Romantic treatment of the tramp life fell into two categories, the first celebrating the supposed freedom of itineracy, and the second lamenting the tragic aspects of this life. The contrast between the two traditions is captured by these tramp songs from around the turn of the century:

> O'er vale and hill I roam at will/ I come at no man's call; /A fetterless tramp with the world for a camp/ Monarch and lord of all.

And

> Tramping, tramping on life's road I go/ No time for grief I cannot weep/ As tramping on I go (Thorpe (1908) and Travers (1892); in Rose, 1988:106).

By the inter-war years the two sub-genres had blended into one, with Merle Haggard's famous *Underneath the Arches* song about Lambeth tramps capturing a bitter-sweet and melancholic sense of live lived on the margins:

> Pavements is my pillow, no matter where I stay, underneath the arches I dream my life away (Rose, 1988:107).

This romantic tradition resonated with the undercurrent of sympathy for the vagrant that was evident during the years of the Depression. Undoubtedly the genre was influenced by aristocratic and bourgeois voyeurs fascinated by the supposed exoticism of underclass life, but there was also a strong sense among the mainly working-class consumers of these popular cultural forms that they themselves were perhaps only one or two steps away from destitution. Many real-life vagrants found that subsistence was made easier if they were able to conform to the newly-emerging romantic notions of tramps as eccentric 'knights of the road' or 'gentlemen tramps'. An important consideration here was the need to become a character by dressing in a distinctive manner and acquiring a sobriquet. An enduring feature of street life from Tudor times onwards, such use of nicknames serves both to encourage a sentimental sympathy for the vagrant and to designate them as outsiders: sympathy may be bought, but at a price.

In a different vein, some contributions to this literary tradition adopted an idealised view of the ennobling nature of vagabond life. Inspired perhaps by Matthew Arnold's poem *The Scholar Gypsy*, Lilian Winstanley's *The Scholar Vagabond* (1909) is set in idyllic rural Wales in midsummer and provides a poetic view of the landscape and way of life of the Welsh-speaking northern region of the country. The hero remains nameless throughout most of the novel, referred to simply as 'the stranger' or 'the man', and is presented throughout as a gentleman and a scholar (his identity as Henry Neobard - this surname translates as 'new Celtic poet' - is only revealed in the penultimate pages). The author teases the reader with the contradictions between these incontrovertible facts and his present condition:

> his boots were the boots of the typical tramp, well worn and dusty, and his coat pockets bulged out behind as if, like the tramp, he carried all his worldly possessions in them ... but his face was refined and thoughtful ... a man probably educated (Winstanley, 1909:2).

This 'stranger' is a wanderer who has lived in South Africa, England and North America before coming to North Wales. He has been a cowboy and policeman as well as a scholar at Oxford, but is now content to seek farmwork during his travels in Wales. During his wanderings, he meets several archetypal characters: Meirion, a poetic youth reciting Celtic and

61

druidic poems and legends; Meirion's honest farming family, the Lloyd-Davies; Ceridwen, Meirion's betrothed who takes her name from the legendary Celtic seer; and Eva who Henry marries and with whom he finally adopts a settled life. Winstanley makes an interesting and clear distinction between the chosen vagabondage of Henry Neobard ('I am used to a wild life and a wild country') and that of Eva Davies, the foundling whom he takes at first to be a gypsy:

> .. this girl had been made homeless and nameless by fate ... if she were a nomad at all, it was by compulsion, and not by choice: she had not the wanderer's instinct (Winstanley, 1909:108).

The dramatic tension of the novel lies in its arousal of the reader's curiosity as to the nature of the hero: is he a gentleman and scholar, or a rogue and vagabond? The characters are drawn from classic formulations, but are by no means crude stereotypes: the novel provides a portrait of a gently rustic landscape, peopled by relatively complex characters. Unusually, a romantic perspective is taken on both the vagabond and the domestic ways of life, with the hero and heroine equally happy within the simplicity of home life and on the open road.

Tramp authors

The genre established by the tramp authors flourished throughout the 19th and early 20th centuries, and their claim to authority was unique in that they themselves could claim to have experienced the tramping life in all its vagaries and vicissitudes. Their aims were variously to instruct, to entertain and to evangelise. Some of these authors were genuine vagrants who happened to have become educated and thus to enter into print. The larger number, however, were middle-class authors who temporarily entered into tramping in order to research the subject, although some wholly fictionalised their accounts without ever leaving their own homes. Some texts presented a gritty social realism, while others were closer to the romantic tradition: W.H. Davies for example 'was a lyric tramp who certainly deodorised, even romanticised, his portrayal of the life-style he had chosen' (Rose, 1988:103). Other commentators were harsher in their judgement of this tramp author:

> Davies was a shopkeeper writ very small ... with a miniature respectability ... the immunisation of the author to the sense of vagrant life ... he thinks like a shopkeeper ... Reality haunted him, and his tramps are ghostly, though well camouflaged in their proper actions (O'Connor, 1963:102).

While Davies' main aim was to entertain, others sought to evangelise and many religious tracts and pamphlets appeared during the 19th century, only thinly disguised as the memoirs or autobiographies of vagrants. *The Memoirs of Mary Saxby* (c.1801) tell the story of a woman living a vagrant life and travelling with gypsies who is convicted of prostitution and sentenced to whipping and a term in the bridewell. Saxby duly undergoes a

Christian conversion, repenting of her 'proud, perverse spirit' and of having been a 'daring rebel'. Ironically, her new found Christianity allows her to continue the wandering life she loves, although now under the guise of a 'respectable' evangelist distributing religious tracts (Golden, 1992).

The Autobiography of a Beggar Boy by James Dawson Burn was first published anonymously in 1855, doubtless to aid the author's claim to authenticity for what is almost certainly a fictionalised work (it was later published under his own name in 1882). Interestingly, Burn dismisses most contemporary fiction as either over-sentimental or else distorted and corrupting. The pseudo-factual style of his work more closely fits his requirements for the written medium to be moral in content and uplifting in tone, and he believed that in contrast to fiction 'biography forms the most pleasing part of history' (Burn, 1855:1)

Clearly written by an educated man, *The Autobiography of a Beggar Boy* aims at the religious and moral instruction of young men. Consisting of a series of letters addressed to 'Thomas', the work gains dramatic appeal from its intimate and personalised account of a man's life over a period of fifty years, and from the sense of immediacy and authenticity derived from the autobiographical genre. Despite Burn's rejection of the fictional style, his book is not unlike much of the picaresque literature in its recounting of multifarious adventures, occasional episodes of good luck and frequent reversals of fortune. In the preface the author promises a work both confessional and naturalistic in style:

> The Author has endeavoured to open up the whole volume of his mind, and thereby expose its most secret springs ... the narrative will be found to be a series of natural incidents ... the Author has made no attempt to either heighten their colour, or enhance their importance (Burn, 1855: iv).

At the same time, the story to be told is one of 'a life full of hardships and romantic adventures'.

The anonymous hero lives a wandering life in England, Scotland and Northern Ireland, suffering physical privation and emotional neglect. He, along with his mother and stepfather, lives variously by begging and by peddling goods and he is beaten frequently by a stepfather who epitomises the evils of intemperance. At intervals, the hero finds an improved situation only to lose it to the force of circumstance: again and again he returns to the vagrant life, until finally his strength of character and his temperance lead him to marriage, fatherhood and a settled domestic life:

> I entirely escaped the leading vice of the ... time, which was intemperance ... The soothing pleasures and quiet enjoyments of home have always exercised a pleasing influence over my mind ... The battle of my life is well calculated to prove to young men what energy and determination of character will accomplish when rightly directed (Burn, 1855:198-99).

Burn thus expresses a major theme within the Victorian and Edwardian rogue literature: the evils of alcohol and the virtues of temperance. He also owes a debt to the earlier rogue pamphleteers in terms of his descriptions of the canting tongue, and in his classification of beggars and vagabonds. He tells us for example that there is an 'aristocracy' among beggars, with the highflyer looking down on the scranbag and the charity irritator. Scottish and Irish beggars, he continues, lag far behind the 'genteel civilisation' of their English counterparts.

Writing of a period of social and economic upheaval, and displaying some sympathy for the revolutionary potential of the newly-urbanising working-classes, Burn's tone is by turns humorous, romantic and moralising. The lightly ironic description of the rookeries of St. Giles as 'that Sylvan retreat where the motley inhabitants spoke all tongues' (p.18) turns later to the expression of a romantic attachment to place: 'In the course of my vagrant wanderings on the Borders, I had learned much of its legendary lore, and romantic history' (p.32). In the end, however, his evangelistic style dominates and this work can be read primarily as a Christian tract, partly disguised as autobiography and social commentary.

In *Children of the Dead End* (1914; reprinted 1985), Patrick MacGill presents the account of his own life story. Subtitled *The Autobiography of a Navvy*, MacGill underlines its authenticity in the foreword to his work:

> most of my story is autobiographical. Moleskin Joe and Carroty Dan are true to life; they live now ... in some evil-smelling lodging house, or, as suits these gypsies of labour, on the open road ... While asking a little allowance for the pen of the novelist it must be said that nearly all the incidents of the book have come under the observation of the writer (MacGill, 1985: xii).

Such claims are supported by John Burnett who, in his introduction to the 1985 edition, accepts that the hero Dermod Flynn's story of migration from the rural north of Ireland to the life of a tramp and a navvy in the lowlands and highlands of Scotland is an accurate reflection of MacGill's own biography. Despite the intimate detail and compelling style that suggests a long and close association with the tramp life, an unresolved question is how this barely-schooled young man could suddenly acquire, as Burnett concedes:

> a knowledge of syntax, a sophisticated vocabulary, a considerable sense of style and powers of imagery after years of hunger, brutal labour and tramping, hardly calculated to provide the basis of a professional literary career (ibid:vi).

Given the relative lack of documentation of MacGill's life, we can only speculate whether he was indeed a self-educated tramp and navvy as he claimed, or whether he was in fact an educated man who temporarily took to the tramping life: wherever the truth lies MacGill's work is an important one in many ways. At a time when poverty and homelessness were increasingly becoming understood as urban phenomena, MacGill contributes a story of the rural itinerant life; and fifty years before radical sociologists began 'telling it like it is', he offered this account, not as a romantic voyeur, but as one of the 'children of the dead end'. He related a sympathetic story of the women and men he encountered, rather than seeking to moralise or evangelise.

MacGill's book is a curious mixture of realism and romanticism, marking the transition between the romantic tendencies of the Victorian and Edwardian tramp authors and the social realist documentary style popular later in the 20th century. The chapter on 'padding it' captures the grim reality of the tramping life :

> Out on tramp, homeless in a strange country, with twopence in my pocket! The darkness lay around me and the snow was white on the ground. Whenever I took my hands out of my pockets the chill air nipped them like pincers. One knee was out through my trousers and my boots were leaking (ibid:92).

This contrasts sharply with his story of the 'open road' which portrays a mystical identification of the tramp with nature :

> I was close to the earth, almost part of it, and the smell of the wet was heavy in my nostrils. It was the breath of the world, the world that was in the eternal throes of change all around me ... winds were moving to and fro with the indecision of homeless wayfarers (ibid:164).

MacGill describes the social exclusion of the tramp, not as the key to some personal freedom, but as creating a painful sense of otherness. For him, tramps are shunned as lepers, children hide behind their mothers on their approach, and they live a lonely life 'shunned and despised by all men, and foul in the eyes of all women' (p.154). No-one offers the tramp a welcome, and his fate is even more bleak than Christ at Calvary as 'the poor tramp is seldom followed even by a mother's prayers along the road where he carries the cross of brotherly hate to the Valley of the Shadow of Death' (p.154). Such suffering serves to ennoble the tramp, rendering him, not the bogeyman of the popular imagination, but someone superior in his sensibilities and compassion :

> My house for so long has been the wide world, that I can afford to look leniently on all other inmates, animal or human. Four walls coffin the human sympathies (ibid:166).

MacGill's compassion extends to the figure of the prostitute woman, so often established as the female counterpart of the male tramp. The Tudor and Stuart doxies and bawdy-baskets were vagrant women assumed almost always (with the exception of the as yet 'unbroken' dells) to be promiscuous in their sexuality, or to be actively engaged in prostitution. This is a theme, certainly not a new one at the time of the rogue pamphlets, that has continued unbroken up until present times. MacGill, however, sought not to reform or to sermonise, but to establish sympathy for the naivety of the countrywoman that led her into contact with 'the evils of prostitution'. Dermod Flynn meets with Norah Ryan in Glasgow, and realises the nature of his love for her :

> It was a love without any corporal end ... To me Norah represented a poetical ideal: she was a saint, the angel of my dreams ... my love for Norah was different. To me she represented a youthful ideal which was too beautiful and pure to be degraded by anything in the world (ibid:268).

This was a radical departure from contemporary literary tradition and popular sensibilities and MacGill presents this romantic version perhaps as a corrective to the prevalent tendency to judge and to condemn.

The philanthropists and social realists

Flourishing from the mid-19th century to the inter-war years, the third genre was that established by a group of aristocratic and bourgeois philanthropists, who combined literary talent with Christian social concern and an active philanthropy. The primary method of investigation of these 'social explorers' can be described as 'going undercover', masquerading as homeless in order to obtain direct experience of the vagrant life (Keating, 1976). Their works were documentary and social scientific in style, but can also be read as fictional or semi-fictional texts in that they sought to entertain as well as instruct. Stephen Graham, a contemporary reviewer of *In Darkest London,* noted that Ada Chesterton's (1926) work 'can be read from end to end as easily as a good novel'.

Many of these philanthropists were concerned with the plight of homeless women, who during this period were emerging from the shadows to become complex characters in their own right, in contrast to their former appearance as two-dimensional companions of the male vagrant. A number of writers paid close attention to the homeless woman, with styles ranging from Charles Dickens' rather preachy factual account of his own *Home for Homeless Women* (1853), to Ada Chesterton's vivid and novelistic story of the *Women of the Underworld* (1928).

Charles Dickens is well known for his portrayal of the underside of London life: indeed, as a socially concerned writer he may be said to be emblematic of his times in the way that Francis Gay was in an earlier century. The homeless, orphaned and destitute child recurs throughout his work, with Oliver Twist as the archetypal impoverished yet innocent child who becomes entrapped in a life of crime. With regard to women, for Dickens as for many of his contemporaries, homelessness was more or less synonymous with prostitution. This was at least partly grounded in reality in that the sexual servicing of men was one of the few means of subsistence for homeless women, but was also a reflection of the age-old association between female vagrancy and sexual deviance. In Dickens' time homeless women simply became conflated with the 'fallen woman'.

The figure of the female prostitute appears frequently in Dickens' work - Nancy in *Oliver Twist*, Edith Dombey in *Dombey and Son* and Martha

Endell in *David Copperfield* - yet it is Dickens' lesser known journalism that is of most interest here. For it is in his anonymous writings in *Household Words* that Dickens allows his first-hand knowledge to inform his prose, whereas his fictional accounts remain rather more removed from experience: 'Dickens himself thought highly of the impossible paragons in his novels, as he did, also, of his pathetic waifs and his melodramatic fallen women' (Collins, 1962:115).

Dickens based his article *Home for Homeless Women* on his own involvement in administering Miss Coutts' Urania Cottage, a home in Shepherd's Bush for around a dozen 'fallen women'. Residents were an eclectic mix of ex-prostitutes, ex-prisoners, destitute girls and ex-inmates of Elizabeth Fry refuges and the Magdalen laundries. Dickens himself made a particular point of interviewing all prospective inmates of Urania Cottage, who were often women he had met 'in the course of my nightly wanderings into strange places' (ibid:111). Once inside the home as voluntary residents, women were offered a reformatory regime based on the ideas of the penal reformer Captain Maconochie, a regime which consisted of domestic work, study and bourgeois pursuits such as gardening and music. The home was run as a Christian institution and marriage was held out as the principal avenue of moral reform, with many of the women also being prepared for emigration to the colonies.

Dickens shared his literary concern with the 'Great Social Evil' of prostitution with writers such as Kingsley, Trollope and Collins, and was undoubtedly heavily influenced by the patriarchal sexual mores of his day. Unlike other novelists, he had direct knowledge of working with prostitute women, but strangely did not allow this to be reflected in his fictional work. As a philanthropist he chose to remain anonymous, ostensibly on the grounds of modesty, but perhaps also because this anonymity allowed him to express his views on the homeless prostitute woman rather more bluntly than in the fictional work published in his own name. For in practice, the 'fallen woman' was not always susceptible to moral reform, and this was a cause of considerable frustration to Dickens. Of a young woman named Sesina he wrote that she was :

> ... the pertest, vainest ... and most deceitful little minx in this town - I never saw such a draggled piece of fringe upon the skirts of all that is bad ... I think she would corrupt a Nunnery in a fortnight (Johnson, 1953:153-5).

Perhaps one of the most famous philanthropists at the turn of the century was Mary Higgs, who was concerned with the moral protection of homeless women, and with the physical conditions endured by both sexes. Her classic *My Brother the Tramp* (1914) works both as a Christian-inspired document on vagrancy and social welfare, and as a social scientific work reviewing legal, cultural, media, and literary discourses on vagrancy. This text outlines Christian duty towards the vagrant and includes scholarly appendices on legal and social aspects of vagrancy, but Higgs nevertheless allows herself some literary embellishment, quoting freely from both media reports and the tramp authors. In this way *My Brother the Tramp* provides an invaluable record of contemporary representations of the tramp and the vagrant. Consistent with the impulse to classify found among many chroniclers of vagrancy, Higgs is careful to distinguish between the 'tramp' and the 'vagrant'. The tramp is the navvy and the itinerant labourer and is thus essential to the economy, but:

> the vagrant is the man who habitually leads a nomadic life (often hereditary) or by reversion (often by compulsion) to the nomadic state ... we need to cut off the supply of vagrants (Higgs, 1914:10).

Contemporaneous media reports favoured vivid descriptions of the tramping life, and especially popular were verbatim accounts from tramps themselves. Higgs cites many such extracts, undoubtedly to express social concern, but also to arouse the attention of the reader, and to lend authenticity to her account. For example:

> It is often said among tramps, 'Don't go to prison for begging: steal, you'll be better treated and stand a chance of being helped when you come out' (*Bath Herald* 18/1/12; in Higgs, 1914:15).

and

> The first time I went on tramp was because I had a sort of nervous breakdown. I could not face up to the day's work and the master, and the quiet of the hedges called me. It's twelve years since then (*Daily News* nd; ibid:20).

Higgs observed a hardening of media attitudes towards the tramp and believed that this was caused by a tightening of the legislation in relation to begging, in particular the institution of the 'way ticket system'. To illustrate her point Higgs cites a *Globe* reporter :

> During a 300-mile walking tour ... the writer was not once accosted by a beggar. The old sociability is dead, crushed by the fear of arrest for mendicancy. The men have become sullen, dispirited, furtive (ibid:54).

Higgs was committed to 'amateur tramping' as a method of social investigation, holding that it allowed her to get closer to understanding 'the life'. Indeed, she was so successful in her undercover disguise that she was once mistaken for a 'hardened old vagrant' by a workhouse official. She was strongly influenced in her work by Christian tradition, in particular the mendicant orders such as the Franciscans who embraced poverty as a religious ideal: 'there in the rags is the community with Jesus. *He became a tramp*' (Higgs, 1914:78, emphasis in original). She refers also to the 'literary tramps' or 'amateur casuals' such as W.H. Davies and the 'tramp parson' Reverend Edwards as being among the few who participated in a 'wave of sympathy' towards the tramp, in contrast to the majority of her contemporaries who allied themselves instead with a 'wave of repression'.

Like Higgs before her, Ada Chesterton went undercover in order to investigate the conditions experienced by the homeless, choosing to focus on women widowed by the Great War. Chesterton believed that female vagrants suffered even worse treatment than their male counterparts and felt they were also more liable to be morally endangered, arguing that they were more sensual, less rational and more sexually promiscuous than men. Like Higgs, Chesterton linked her socially concerned writing with a practical philanthropy, and worked to establish women's model lodging-houses, in an era when there was virtually no separate provision for homeless women, outside of institutions for moral rescue.

In her novelistic style, Chesterton takes the reader with her on a tour of the West End of London, using the device of her service to the homeless of food and drink from a 'perambulatory coffee-stall' as a means of observing the homeless in their habitual haunts. She captures the dramatic tension between the surface affluence of the capital of the British Empire, and the underworld existence of its poor and homeless:

> It is at night that the homeless, the hungry and the hopeless of London's underworld come to the surface ... through the sombre hours between darkness and dawn they emerge into existence ... from every side shadowy forms, rising from half-concealed benches, closed in on us (Chesterton 1928:195-7).

Chesterton herself has a 'queer adventure' while attempting to sleep rough in Hyde Park: for a time she evades detection but is eventually intercepted and moved on by the police, finding that she was required, along with all other vagrants, to leave the park between the hours of midnight and 5 am. It is difficult to determine whether her characters are fictional or biographical, but Chesterton presents them all in colourful and sympathetic language. She is systematic in her observations but is more romantic and less scholarly than Higgs, describing one woman as a:

> ... native of the underworld ... I like to think of that old sportswoman holding her own against the cold, against hunger and against authority. She wants freedom and is prepared to pay for it ... Who could find it in their hearts to break my vagrant friend's lone fight for liberty? (ibid:209-11).

While Chesterton's approach is a broadly Christian one she is not given to the careful exegesis of Higgs: rather her philosophy may be summed up by the simple aphorism 'there but for the grace of God go I'. Although her views on the sexual morality of female vagrants were clearly influenced by contemporary social and media constructions, she was nevertheless aware that the apparent security and prosperity of the middle-class woman was almost entirely dependent on her attachment to a prosperous male, and that widowhood could (and frequently did) bring with it destitution. Finally, hers was a compassionate vision, one that accorded full human complexity to the often dehumanised underclass of her times: 'there is light and shade, humour and endurance in this underworld' (ibid:219).

From social realism to post-modern fiction

The postwar literature of homelessness can be characterised by one predominant theme: the persistence of premodern homelessness into modern or post-modern times, highlighting the stark evidence of abject need amidst affluence. This concern has been given expression within a variety of media, and the favoured investigative technique of going undercover has persisted into the late twentieth century.

The early 1960s was an interesting period of transition between the Christian philanthropy of the preceding century, and the social documentary genre of succeeding decades. Philip O'Connor (1963) continued the established tradition of taking to the roads as a tramp, and identified himself as 'Mr Other'. His now classic work on vagrancy is part autobiography and part social commentary, inspired by the author's Christian socialist beliefs, and written in an unusual stream-of-consciousness style.

O'Connor's aim was to document the ethos of the tramp and the vagrant whom he tends to romanticise as anti-materialist heroes in the Franciscan tradition: 'the tramp ... is the rebel against the bourgeois-Calvinist precept that all must work' (1963:133). Like Higgs before him, he notes that St. Francis and Christ himself could be understood as tramps and beggars. At one level his concern is with the material welfare of vagrants, and he is one of the first postwar commentators to note the contradiction posed by the fact of poverty among plenty :

> Tramping does, of course, pull one back centuries; emotion about food and shelter is old fashioned ... Security and plenty are utterly modern - futuristic, even (ibid:137).

However, his concern is equally with spiritual matters, and he sees the act of wandering as an escape from both self and society. Continual motion is both physically and mentally numbing, and the vagrant thus becomes freed from ego in the way of the wandering saints. For the itinerant, time takes on a cyclical rather than linear dimension. O'Connor recognises that each age tends to romanticise the vagrants of a former era, yet he himself adopts a semi-mystical view of the vagabond life:

> The tramp is on a road, and the road is a symbol, and tramping is metaphorical ... So basic a metaphor of human progress is tramping that it is a pilgrimage neither of the body nor of the soul, but a prescientific and antique integration of both (ibid:79).

Such sentiments probably express more about the hopes and longings of the author than about the experiences of most men and women on the road.

The 1960s and 1970s saw the development of a striking new televisual genre, the docudrama, whose dramatic sequences and black-and-white air of gritty realism were perfectly suited to the subject of homelessness. This period also witnessed a shift in focus from the 'old' homelessness of the tramp, the vagrant and the middle-aged alcoholic, towards an awareness of 'new' homeless groups such as women, families and younger people. *Edna the Inebriate Woman* (1976) told the story of the often-forgotten homeless woman, *Cathy Come Home* (1966) famously documented the disintegration of homeless families within the modern welfare state, while *Johnny Go Home* (1975) controversially followed the 'dilly boys' into the 'twilight world' of youth homelessness and male prostitution. The voice-over of the latter docudrama explicitly contrasted notions of Victorian poverty and squalor with the glitter of modern, affluent society:

> Tommy's new found friends rapidly introduce him to the twilight world of Piccadilly ... In the heat of an improvised bonfire in the old Covent Garden, the kids, the drifters and the down-and-outs gather in a way that's hardly changed since Dickens time (Beresford, 1979:156).

The medium of television was to become an increasingly important one during the 1970s and 1980s, and the investigative journalism style of the docudramas came to influence literature of many kinds, both factual and fictional. In turn the narrative drama of fictional work, and the conventions of popular autobiography were both adopted to great effect by television dramas. One very successful and much imitated example was Tony Wilkinson's (1981) account of his experiences of being down and out:

> It was something new in television documentaries: a fictional character in a real world, a television reporter's eye in the body of an inarticulate derelict (Wilkinson,1981:7).

New to television this may have been, but Wilkinson's story (also told in his book) contained all the familiar elements established in Victorian and Edwardian times: the device of going undercover, the narrative drama and authenticity of an autobiographical account, combined with strong elements of social concern and human interest. As always, the combination of a sympathetic 'there but for the grace of god' identification with the homeless and legitimised voyeurism proved irresistible to the audience.

Wilkinson described his work as belonging to a radical tradition and was careful to underline its authentic and documentary nature: 'their language is the raw talk of the streets rather than the novelist's highly wrought reconstruction of what might have been said' (ibid:7). He went undercover for one month on the streets of London, followed by a film crew also in disguise. In the tradition of many ethnographers, he offers a reflexive account of his adoption of a new persona:

> ... it was not going to be like an actor taking to the stage for a few hours and then being able to return home to warmth and friends ... It was more like being a spy ... I did not want to be this other person, this charmless inarticulate, this dosser (ibid:11-12).

Almost predictably, the author discovered that 'the workhouse of Charles Dickens' day still existed' (p.8), and less surprisingly still that 'the freedoms he expected from his irresponsible lifestyle never materialized' (p.9). The characters that he encountered on the streets were the familiar ones of prostitutes, drunken men and tramp preachers, although we see the addition of new homeless groups such as skinheads and 'spike-haired punks'. The antique distinction between the deserving (those unemployed and homeless 'through no fault of their own') and the undeserving ('inadequates ... derelicts ... and failures') was also made. In short, little about Wilkinson's perspective, methodology or thesis was new: the only new element was the medium in which his work was presented, and the mass audiences it was thus able to reach.

Into the 1990s we discover that the literature of homelessness and crime is as diverse and as popular as ever. Homelessness itself has been discovered and rediscovered as a social problem countless times during the postwar period, and it might be thought that there was by now little left to say. Two books published in the same year, however, succeeded in finding different ways of telling what is in essence a very old story. Chris Kitch's (1996) autobiography provides a portrayal of the classic vagabond-scholar and is written in a familiar part-confessional and part-social documentary style, yet as a woman she provides a rare account of the female criminal anti-hero.

Ruth Rendell, (the 'queen of crime fiction'), published her novel *Keys to the Street* in the same year as Kitch her autobiography, at a time when street homelessness was being criminalised by legislators and demonised by the press. Rendell's achievement has been to capture the uneasy sense in which premodern and post-modern forms of homelessness happen to co-exist and to incorporate a myriad of literary and mythical references to the figure of the vagabond.

Kitch's *Pavement for my Pillow* establishes a clear association with the tramping tradition, taking its title from the popular song of the inter-war years: *Underneath the Arches*. Kitch is unusual in being a female tramp author but her story is not unfamiliar. Neglected and mistreated as a child, she spent time in borstals and women's prisons, before entering into a life of prostitution, drug abuse and early motherhood, and finally slipping into many years spent on the streets. Her childhood sense of herself as an outsider because of her 'bastard' birth was compounded in adulthood by her alienation from society as a lesbian woman.

Kitch's story continues with her escape from the streets, following which she underwent drug rehabilitation programmes, rediscovered Christianity, regained her physical fitness and entered higher education. She became a minor celebrity and began to be recognised in the streets following the television version of her autobiography: *Raising Lazarus*. The chronological impetus of such autobiographical work lends itself to the metaphor of the journey, a particularly commonplace and evocative device within the literature of homelessness:

> I feel as if I have spent myself in the telling of this tale, this tale of a journey which is not over, of a journey that has within it many journeys and is only part of a much bigger journey ... The end of the story is but the beginning of the story (Kitch, 1996:197).

In *The Keys to the Street* Ruth Rendell deals with many of the same questions as Kitch, with both authors telling of the mixing of old and new forms of homelessness, with for example the 'jacks men' co-existing with the younger 'junkies'. However, the similarity between the two works is confined largely to content: in terms of style Kitch's straightforward autobiography contrasts with Rendell's complex and meticulously researched fiction in which she explores multi-layered notions of homelessness. The 'keys to the street' are the innumerable keys collected by the psychopath Clancy, and worn by him like a suit of armour: 'having no home, he had collected keys to the homes of others, keys being the symbol of home ownership, of possession and of the privacy he could no longer enjoy' (Rendell, 1996:218).

A secondary but perhaps more pervasive motif is that of the railings in the Park where the street people sleep: 'there are railings everywhere, their spikes straight and pointed, twisted at a right angle or ornate and blunted' (ibid: 2). The railings are the element that by turn contains, excludes, protects - yet finally serves to kill - the homeless. For those who live in (rather than merely visit) the Park are stalked by the Impaler, a serial killer who claims the homeless as his victims and brutally leaves their bodies on the spikes of the railings. In this way Rendell gives fictional expression to the notion of the homeless person as victim, a notion that, as we shall see in chapter five, has scarcely entered into popular, media or academic consciousness:

> Who would be next? Would it be one of them? ... Roman fancied they were more subdued than usual, more wary. They, who had never been afraid of what people with roofs over their heads feared, the streets, the dark, were afraid of them now (ibid:224).

Rendell's portrayal of homeless people is both subtle and complex. She finds inspiration in earlier literary and cultural traditions and compares homeless people variously with the Wandering Jew, Oedipus and the holy fool. The central character is set apart from those made homeless by circumstance or by defect of character (for even in Rendell there is a distinction between the 'deserving' and the 'undeserving'): Roman is the singular person who has chosen homelessness as an escape from personal tragedy. Echoing *King Lear*, Rendell tells us that:

> He had become unacccommodated man, perhaps even what those existentialists said man should be - free, suffering, alone, and in control of his own destiny (ibid:41).

Thus, even within the most recent and most sophisticated literature, the concept of the romantic nomad persists and we find echoes of the vagabond-scholar and the tragi-melancholic tramp. Finally, Rendell portrays the homeless as shadow figures, as people occupying the spaces between social worlds but never quite belonging anywhere:

> Street people, no matter what they wear, or what they started off wearing, always seem to be dressed in darkness. They are blackened, everything muted by time and dirt to the colour of shadows... (ibid:295).

From Shakespeare to contemporary crime fiction, literature has concerned itself with the liminality and existential freedom of homelessness, and it is to the 'unaccommodated woman' that we now turn our attention.

4 The unaccommodated woman

> Thou wert better in a grave, than to answer with/ thy uncover'd body, this extremity of the skies ... /Thou art the thing itself; unaccommodated man, is/ no more but such a poor, bare, forked animal as thou art./ Off, off you lendings: come, unbutton here (*King Lear*, Shakespeare, 1606, Act 3, Scene IV, lines 108-15).

Lear, driven to madness in part by the perceived ingratitude of his daughter Cordelia, comes to embrace homelessness in an attempt to become the simple man represented by Tom O'Bedlam, the metaphor of the Elizabethan beggar that recurs throughout the play. In so doing he both abhors ('thou wert better in a grave') and embraces ('come, unbutton here') the conditions of poverty and homelessness. Such ambivalence is evoked by the simultaneous fear of material privation and the lure of existential simplicity and freedom from social constraint. The dual attraction and repulsion of homelessness continues to affect the modern imagination.

To paraphrase Shakespeare, the 'unaccommodated woman' is the homeless woman, one who is literally without accommodation. She can also be understood as the woman who does not or cannot accommodate herself to social convention. Alternatively, it is the social world that does not or cannot bring itself to accommodate its outcast women. Thus, unaccommodated women - the homeless, single mothers, battered and abused women, women working the streets - have not accepted, or sometimes have been refused, their place in the world.

This chapter explores the gendered meanings of home and homelessness, the social and spatial ordering of the home in relation to the construction of identity, the experience of home-as-prison among many 'homeless-at-home' women, and ways of becoming and being homeless. Women have appeared only as shadows within the legislative and literary discourses of homelessness discussed in the previous two chapters, yet paradoxically home is central to a woman's experience in a way not commonly shared by men. In a sense, home is so closely identified with women that the homeless woman becomes an anomaly, someone so deviant that she *can* exist only within the shadows.

> ..in a sense, without homelessness, we would not be concerned with what home means (Dovey, 1985:48).

'Home' and 'homelessness' are not simple descriptions of 'being in the world': they refer, rather, to complex and shifting experiences and identities. The concept of home, as opposed to the physical reality of a house, could not exist without homelessness, just as, in a Durkheimian sense, conformity cannot exist without deviance. Homelessness, then, serves to define and delineate home, in a dynamic and dialectic fashion.

From a phenomenological perspective, 'being at home' is an unselfconscious and taken-for-granted state: to be homeless brings with it an awareness of absence, a consciousness of difference, of deviation from the norm. Home has been represented as a series of binary opposites: as a place of rest after a journey has been undertaken, as a private retreat from the public world, and as a familiar and secure space within a strange and insecure world . It is this dialectic tension between such binary opposites that gives meaning both to 'home' and to 'homelessness' (Dovey, 1985). There is, however, a danger in such a 'happy phenomenology of the home' (Sibley, 1995:94). Tension between the binary opposites of safety and risk, security and fear, privacy and invasion may exist *within* the home for many, in contrast to simplified and idealised notions of domestic space. Many homeless young people have grown up in Homes rather than a private home, while others are 'domestic refugees' from violent situations (Martin, 1987).

Furthermore, distinctions between home and homelessness may break down in particular circumstances, in that individuals do not passively respond to apparently objective reality, but negotiate their own identities. To counterpoint two cases discussed in more detail below, Katy could be described as 'homeless at home', given her lack of any sense of home while living with her family, while Ruksana, contrary to all official designations of those living in hostels as 'homeless', could declare that she did not consider herself to be homeless.

These qualifications notwithstanding, the understanding of home and homelessness as binary opposites has relevance on two counts: first, the romantic tradition within the homelessness literature, discussed at length in the previous chapter, is based on a neglect of an understanding that the excitement of the journey, so attractive and evocative to the usually male and middle-class academic, becomes much less so when there is no home to which to return (Anderson, 1923; Kennedy, 1983). Romantic notions of journeying have usually been premised on the assumption of escape from domesticity, and therefore (by implication) the masculine escape from a female domain (Cohen and Taylor, 1992; Gordon, 1991; Wolff, 1993). The male romance of the open road contrasts sharply with female terror at the dangers inherent in the journey, although Kaler (1991) provides us with a rare account of the female *picara* as 'fantasy heroine'. Furthermore, a 'home' with no 'journey' becomes a prison, in that the home may serve as a source of order and identity, but with no opposite, no 'outside', the individual becomes constrained and confined.

The meaning of home

> *home*:   the place where one lives; a dwelling-house; the members of a family collectively; the native land of a person or a person's ancestors; an institution for persons needing care, rest or refuge; the place where a thing originates or is most common (Concise Oxford Dictionary, 1991).

'Home' can mean private abode or public institution, it can be a place of refuge or a prison. Whatever home is, popular wisdom tells us that 'a house is not a home', such that home is understood to not only involve a physical arrangement of space, but also an expression of social meanings and identities. A *house* represents conceptual space, it is abstract, rational, geometric. *Home* is an expression of lived space, of human meaning and being-in-the-world (Dovey, 1985; Heidegger, 1962).

Home may be the suburban semi-detached dream, a tower-block apartment or a room of one's own in an institutional home. We have our 'home' towns and cities, homelands, tribal or otherwise, real or imagined, as well as spaces designated as the centre of a people or nation (such as the 'Home Counties'). These many meanings of home are possible precisely because 'home' is not anchored in physical space. Home is at least partially a physical place, but it is more a state of being. A room, a house, a city or a nation may all be understood as home, in dialectical opposition to something larger, something that lies outside and beyond that which is defined as home.

Conversely, spaces generally understood as home may not be experienced as such: the statement that 'I do not have a home' may equally mean that 'I have no house in which to live' or 'the house in which I live does not feel like a home' (Dovey, 1985). Furthermore, a sense of homelessness may be felt by communities and nations as well as individuals, arising from marginalisation, alienation, migrations, expulsions and the creation of national or cultural diasporas (Bammer, 1994). The American South, with its history of enslavement and oppression, has created just such a sense of homelessness and radical alienation among black people:

> At times home is nowhere. At times one knows only extreme estrangement and alienation. Then home is no longer just one place. It is locations. Home is that place which enables and promotes varied and everchanging perspectives, a place where one discovers new ways of seeing reality, frontiers of difference (hooks, 1991:148).

Here, hooks provides us with a positive sense of home, describing its potential to radically enhance individual lives. For her, home is not a private, static, taken-for-granted entity, but something that represents the dynamic interchange between the individual and the world, between inside and outside, private and public, individual and community.

Home and order

> The house is thus a kind of 'book' that is read by the body through its interactions (Dovey, 1985:39).

Phenomenology offers a dialectic perspective on home that counterposes inside with outside spaces. 'Home' or 'inside' is equated with security, certainty, order, family and femaleness, while 'outside' or 'journey' becomes synonymous with risk, strangeness, chaos, masculinity and the public realm (Altman and Werner, 1985). Home is also constructed as a source of both individual and social identity. Psychoanalytic perspectives emphasise the home as a source of personal identity and view the house as a symbolic representation of the body, as do many tribal cultures (Jung, 1967; Cooper, 1974), while almost universally in Western cultures the house is understood as an expression of social identity and status (Saunders, 1981). Rex and Moore's (1967) pioneering work in Birmingham has allowed us to understand some of the different perceptions and meanings of home that may pertain within any particular society, mediated by ethnicity, class and culture.

Alongside this socio-spatial order there exists also a temporal ordering of the home. Repeated physical routines, or 'fields of care', within a *house*, may over time create a sense of *home* (Korosec-Serfaty, 1985). The home thus becomes a source of identity and status, and allows for a sense of connection to both people and places, to the past and to the future. Although there is a degree of flexibility within these perspectives - in that individuals may be creative in where and how they achieve this sense of home - these are nevertheless inherently conservative world views in their assumption that fixed and rooted categories of the social world arise necessarily from an individual's early experiences of home.

Such perspectives offer an understanding of the home as a source of order and identity, but they neglect a wider social analysis. Put simply, traditional concepts of home are based on assumptions of the white, middle-class and heterosexual nuclear family (Wagner, 1993; Passaro, 1996). The widespread nature of violence within families is overlooked, as is the social and spatial exclusion of those who do not fit into the purified space of residential neighbourhoods, spaces that are hardened against marginal people (Davis, 1990; Massey, 1992; Sibley, 1995; Sennett, 1996). Unaccommodated women and men are those 'gender renegades' who are rejected by, and are rejecting of, conventional household structures (Passaro, 1996).

An understanding of home as a 'haven in a heartless world' relies on a rigid separation of inside and outside, with safety and security to be found inside, and fear and danger remaining outside. Such a definition of home can be said to contribute to the creation of homelessness, in that those who are abused and violated within the family are likely to feel 'homeless at home', and many subsequently become homeless in an objective sense, in that they escape - or are ejected from - their violent homes (Dibblin, 1991; Douglas and Gilroy, 1994; Hendessi, 1992). Furthermore, those who are not able to, or choose not to, conform to the gender, class and sexuality deals inherent in establishing a conventional household, find themselves symbolically (and often literally) excluded from any notion or semblance of home (Carlen, 1988; Smailes, 1994). The impulse to exclude and expel deviant others from conventional notions of home and neighbourhood is an essential, although perpetually uncompleted function. The Other is excluded from purified space, but does not cease to exist: they remain present and visible and thus continue to be dangerous. The Other has its own power, the ability to inspire fear (Sibley, 1995).

Home is widely, and often unproblematically, associated with femaleness: both with the women who are expected to maintain hearth and home, and with the presumed feminine principles of boundedness, physicality and nurturance. It should follow, then, that male and female relations to the home will differ radically. Object relations theory, for example, holds that females identify with their mothers (and by implication with home), and thereby establish a sense of connectedness to people and places. It is argued that males from an early age, in contrast, learn to differentiate themselves from mother and home, establish boundaries between themselves and the world, and thus establish a sense of themselves as separate and disconnected (Massey, 1992).

Although this over-simplified and often masculinist understanding of space is the dominant one, and is reflected in much theorising about the home, nevertheless women (and many marginal men) have a more complex relationship to the home. For them, there may be no clear binary divide between home and homelessness, between inside and outside, safety and danger, but rather a more individual and cyclical relation to each of these conditions. Both women and men are likely to experience home and homelessness on a cyclical basis, moving between degrees of relative security and insecurity and experiencing both freedom and confinement at home and on the streets (Fleisher, 1995; Carlen, 1996; Hagan and McCarthy, 1997). In particular, the inside and the outside are not hermetically sealed from each other, but are intimately interconnected. Thus, it is perhaps more meaningful to talk of the 'outside within', the impact of the social world on the spaces and places occupied by people (Massey, 1992).

Home as prison

> Home is not a windowless grave, but a place I may go both in and out of (*About the House*, W.H. Auden, 1966).

> Home is the girl's prison and the woman's workhouse (*Women in the Home*, George Bernard Shaw, 1995).

Katy spent her childhood with a violent mother and sexually abusive stepfather, and described the way in which she was closely confined to the home:

> I couldn't see boyfriends, or see my mates. And when I did go out, I'd just stay on the front of the house. No, he'd [stepfather] want me all to himself (23 year-old white woman, Birmingham hostel).

After leaving home at age sixteen (she refers to this as having 'escaped') and spending three years without a home, Katy was living in a hostel for homeless mothers at the time of interview, and reflected that she could not remember ever having felt 'at home'. Describing her early and middle childhood, she said:

> But I suppose I could have classed myself homeless then, because it wasn't really a home. Yeah, 'cause a home, it's a family, a good family atmosphere, and you do things together. The only time I'd had a family atmosphere is when I was fostered and that was about it.

Equally, she identified the misery of literal homelessness with an almost Dickensian sense of alienation and exclusion: 'One of the worst things about being homeless is at Christmas, seeing families through the window enjoying themselves and thinking "I'm out in the cold".'

Ruksana spent her childhood in Britain and her early adulthood with her family in Pakistan, where she was desperately unhappy:

> My mum couldn't understand it, look we've got a lovely house, we've got servants, we've got everything you could wish for ... But she couldn't understand what I was going through ... after a full day's teaching I'd think 'Oh, I'm going back to that prison, and I hate it' (25 year-old Asian woman, Wolverhampton hostel).

She went on to explain that she only began to experience some of the benefits supposed to attach to home once she had left her parents' house to live in a hostel in the English Midlands:

> I'll tell you something. I've got more privacy here than I got at bloody home. I know once my bedroom door here is closed no-one is going to come in, and if they do come in they're going to knock. I'll sit here reading a letter or writing a letter, no-one will ... at home it's 'what are you writing? Tell us what you're ...' I mean I think I've got more privacy here than what I got at home ... I don't consider myself homeless.

Ruksana contrasted the relative freedoms of homelessness with the restrictions placed on her as a Muslim woman:

> I don't consider myself as an Asian, even though I am ... I've left my community. And to tell [you] the odd thing really, the English community is a very easy community to live in. You can do anything you want and no-one's going to turn around ... and say 'why you doing this, why you doing that?'

She was also acutely aware of her anomalous position as a young Asian woman who had left home outside of the framework of marriage: indeed she had consciously and consistently resisted marriage in an attempt to maintain a measure of independence:

Once you're married, if you don't like your husband you're bloody stuck with him. If you leave your husband and you go back to your parents' house they'll still force you to go back to him. *It's your only place* ... if you get a divorce society is going to spit on you (emphasis added).

Her position as a gender and cultural renegade led her to literal homelessness, but allowed her to create her own notion of home and freedom in a hostel in a Midlands town.

For other women, there was little if any element of choice in their situation: finding themselves homeless was a consequence of the collapse of their dream ideas of home. Shanaz, a thirty year-old woman originally from north-west England and at the time of interview living in a hostel in Wolverhampton, married to escape an abusive and exploitative home life, but exchanged this for years of violence and the eventual loss of her house, home and children. She tells her story:

We had just moved into it ... and I was so happy then, thinking 'Oh I got me house' ... it was my sort of dream house ... I would put flowers in the garden ... not knowing I wasn't going to live in the house ... [we] bought the house in September and in March he [her husband] was really getting worse ... and I picks up the 'phone and goes to my brother 'I need your help now, because I just can't take it no more. *I'm coming home for good. I never want to come back to this place again*' (emphasis added).

Shanaz clearly experienced ambivalent feelings in relation to the question of home: strong emotional links with her mother's house (*home*), contrasted with her marital place of residence, which she described as a *house*, or *this place*. However, she recognised the extreme pressures placed on her to make a home with her husband in order to maintain family *izzat*, or reputation. Once she has left her parents' house, a married (not widowed) Asian woman would find it difficult to return there with her own and her family's reputation intact.

For many women, the home is not primarily a place to return to after a journey, a place of rest and relaxation: rather, it is a place of domestic and emotional labour. Shanaz is one woman who engaged in intensive domestic work from early childhood through to her violent married life. In this part of her story we gain a sense, not only of the labour involved, but also of the degree of control thus exerted over her life:

[At seven or eight] I was left with four brothers, three sisters we were. I was left bringing them up. That was going to school, doing the cooking, them days it was making the coal fire, things like that, cleaning the house ...

Then just turned seventeen, just after a month of marriage, got pregnant. Got married in a family where there were seven sisters and three brothers, a father that's disabled and a mother-in-law that used always stay in bed ... And it was only me doing the work in the house. And I was up from seven in the morning till two in the morning, you know, working for all them.

Then after two or three years of living with me mother-in-law eventually we got a house, which was a dump again ... I used to have everything spotless, do the cooking, do the cleaning, looking after the kids, making sure that everything's right for them ... He'd say 'by the time I come back make sure you get on your hands and knees and scrub them floorboards down there' ... Then I was having a sort of breakdown ... Everyone thinks you're happy because of his acting and me not saying anything to nobody. *But who knows what's going on inside the house?* Only me (emphasis added)

Homeless men are more likely to be able to retain their dreams of domesticity, while homeless women tend to frame their hopes in terms of secure careers and independent accommodation. Ahmad, a 17 year-old Birmingham man, described his hopes in this way:

I know I'm gonna meet a girl one day who's gonna be the girl for me, have kids and that ... twenty years from now I'll be retired with a three-bedroomed house, with kids and a missus and a car ... I'm a bit ambitious but that's what's gonna happen.

His domestic aspirations remained intact despite being a father to a child with whom he had no contact, and despite being prevented by court injunction from contacting his former partner. Such aspirations were unlikely to survive in women who had suffered the shattering of their domestic dreams. Women seemed less capable of such magical thinking, perhaps not surprisingly, given that the costs of maintaining traditional femininities are high and the rewards (unlike those for the maintenance of conventional masculinities) relatively low.

The home, then, has significantly different meanings for women and men: men are encouraged to view it as a domain over which they have control, but to which they contribute little labour. Conversely, women identify with, labour within, and take responsibility for the home, yet have little autonomy within this their sphere. Many still lack a 'room of one's own', still less any control over the ordering of time and space within the home (Woolf, 1929; Darke, 1994).

Ways of being homeless

The paths to homelessness, then, are many. Many young women and men can trace the roots of their homelessness to their experiences of home: family or partnership breakdowns are consistently cited as the most common precipitator of homelessness, with escaping violent situations and leaving institutional care and control also significant factors (Daly, 1996; Hutson and Liddiard, 1994; Stein et al, 1994). Different routes are taken by those women who have experienced themselves to be 'homeless at home', by those gender renegades and transgressors who were unable or unwilling to conform to traditional family forms and norms, and by those whose 'homes' were in effect prison cells. Just as there are many routes to becoming homeless, so there are various ways of being homeless. Here we can explore some of these ways of being homeless, as well as identifying some of the strategies of resistance employed by homeless women to the social spaces and places in which they find themselves located. It is important to capture a sense of agency among such women, but they should not be portrayed as proto-feminist revolutionaries. Some were more or less consciously rejecting gender norms, but others retained an attachment to conventional domesticity and traditional 'family values': these women were, at most, reluctant rebels.

Mainstream traditions of research hold that the homeless population is anomic, retreatist and disaffiliated (Merton, 1968; Bahr and Caplow, 1973), although later interactionist research emphasises the social networks, sense of agency and levels of resistance among homeless populations (Snow and Anderson, 1993; Wagner, 1993). Drawing on the life-stories told by homeless women, two major ways of being (or resisting being) homeless can be identified: the management of body space and identity work.

Managing body space

The body is the most fundamental boundary for the individual, with the skin surrounding the body serving both to define the person and to separate them from their environment. The body assumes paramount importance for the homeless, in that the absence of a home that might serve as a second skin renders the body the first and often only line of defence against a dangerous world. The nature of bodily defensive reaction to the vulnerability of homelessness is of two general types: contraction or expansion. The homeless person may seek either to reduce the visibility of their physical body and the space occupied by it, or else to increase their *umwelt*, their sphere of protection (Goffman, 1971). Women who feel themselves to be 'homeless at home' may respond by becoming anorexic (as in the case of Ruksana), while street homeless women typically disappear into the shadows (Bunston and Breton, 1990; Sibley, 1995; Malson, 1997). Both types of response are about altering (and specifically reducing) their bodily sheaths - the only boundary under their direct control - in order to maximise physical and psychological safety (Goffman, 1971).

Sarah for example did her best to become invisible while living rough on the streets, but still experienced high levels of fearfulness:

> I slept rough but it wasn't really on the streets, it was a derelict building. I did that once and it frightened me. I couldn't sleep, I was awake all night ... I was frightened of closing my eyes because you hear that many horrible things (27 year-old white woman, day centre in Manchester).

Conversely, extension of bodily space is a more frequent masculine response to the dangers of homelessness. The defensive space around a person, within which they are able to perceive and respond to danger, typically expands in public places and contracts within known and safe spaces such as the home

(Goffman, 1971). For those living permanently in public places, there is no safe space within which they can relax their vigilance. Many homeless men choose to expand their *umwelt* to include a wide area of the cityscape, rather than to disappear, and for them safety lies not in the shadows but in claiming the streets as their own.

Certainly, homeless men as well as women become adept at decreasing their public visibility when necessary, and they too are subject to many fears and vulnerabilities. Nevertheless, men can claim a place on the streets in ways that women seldom can, and thus their survival strategies will differ: women must 'disappear' in order to survive, while men have the additional option of seeking safety in numbers, and thereby asserting 'ownership' of some public places. John, a *Big Issue* vendor in Manchester, describes his perspective:

> There were loads of us sleeping out in summer, under the pagoda in Chinatown ... there were about twenty or thirty of us ... anyone can kip anywhere, some people just kip in the [Piccadilly] Gardens, where it's really open ... You hear about this streetwise stuff, and it's not bull or nothing. It's a big bad jungle out there, and you gotta know where you're going and where you stand. I'd never get mugged, not me, 'cause I know too many people, know all the people around town, so I'd never get mugged ... I know how to rough it and I've learnt the way of the town as well ... I've got the knowledge to know I can survive on the street.

None of the women in this study expressed this level of confidence and sureness, even though many could be described as streetwise: few if any sought safety in numbers, or felt able to live and sleep rough as openly as this. In many ways the streets are the quintessential male space, with women maintaining at best an ambivalent relationship with the street.

One peculiarly female version does exist of the strategy of extending physical space in order to maximise personal safety and protection. The 'bag lady' (significantly, there is no male counterpart) carries everywhere with her a collection of objects that come to signify for her a 'mobile home' (Lofland, 1973; Russell, 1991). Laden with belongings, some useful at a material level, others with a more symbolic significance, she thus creates her own sense of home and selfhood. However, the 'bag lady' appears to be an age- as well as gender-related phenomenon, one that is associated almost exclusively with older women. Certainly, none of the young women in my research could be described as a bag lady and on the contrary most carried with them as few possessions as possible.

Identity work

> Our status is backed by the solid buildings of the world, while our sense of personal identity resides in the cracks (Goffman, 1961:320).

Homeless people engage in a range of identity work in an effort to 'salvage the self' (Snow and Anderson, 1993). Two of the most important of these strategies are role distancing and role embracement, in relation to a homeless

84

identity. Such apparently opposite strategies have in common their resistance to role ascription, and their active negotiation of identity. A clear example of role distancing is the case of Ruksana who was able to declare that she was not homeless even while living in a hostel. Katy, in contrast, had felt herself to be homeless-at-home while living with her family. Into adulthood, she had little urge to seek a conventional home of her own, preferring the company and emotional support of hostel life:

> The hostel is an institution, and all the hostels I've been in are institutions, and that's why I don't want my own flat, because I've been institutionalised for so long, three years, and [I've] always depended on people really.

Ambivalently aware of both the advantages and disadvantages of institutional life, the fears and dangers of home life nevertheless persuaded her to embrace her homeless identity.

Ruksana's role distancing and Katy's role embracement appear to be diametrically opposed strategies, but apparent role distancing may obscure an underlying role attachment (Goffman, 1972). Ruksana's self-definition as 'not homeless' represented a distancing from negative attitudes towards the homeless, rather than from her own experience of homelessness per se. As we have seen, Ruksana welcomed her new life in the hostel, representing as it did privacy and self-determination: control over such things as privacy serve to define the boundaries of the self and thus to help construct identity (Altman, 1975).

Furthermore, there is an underlying commonality in that role distancing and role embracement can both represent (more or less successful) attempts by individuals to choose their own location within the home-to-homelessness continuum (Watson with Austerberry, 1986). In their different ways, both Ruksana and Katy were resisting both official definitions and public perceptions of what it means to be homeless. In asserting their own identities they were shaking off the passivity expected of social victims. Within the apparently rigid social and spatial boundaries that delimit homelessness, they succeeded in introducing a degree of flexibility and in establishing some 'free space' for themselves (Goffman, 1961).

The unaccommodated woman

The unaccommodated woman is the deviant Other. The simple fact of her existence outside of the social and spatial boundaries of home, family and domesticity threatens to undermine the construction of the home as a source of identity and as a foundation of social order. Whether they are to be understood as gender renegades or reluctant rebels, such women often become homeless following violence and repression within their homes-as-prison. For some of those who have defined themselves as homeless-at-home, literal homelessness brings with it material deprivation and loss of identity, but it may also represent a degree of freedom, in comparison with their experiences of home as wives and daughters.

Paradoxically, while homelessness may represent a limited sense of freedom for some women, for some of the time, and while it may challenge the confinement of individual women within domestic space, nevertheless homelessness is - in gender terms - an inherently conservative phenomenon on at least two counts. First, homelessness and home, as has been argued above, serve to define and maintain one another, and both states are frequently inimical to the economic, social and cultural autonomy of women. Second, the home-homelessness binary divide serves to underscore the 'goodness' of those women who consent to maintain the home (almost any home will do), and to be contained within this sphere, and the 'badness' of those women (and marginal men) whose only homes are the streets or the non-homes of institutional life. Once having left (or having been expelled from) home, it remains for them to find ways of being homeless, and to begin to find their place in the world.

5 Homelessness and victimisation

This chapter is concerned primarily with the absence of the homeless victim: absent from popular consciousness and the criminal justice system, as well as absent from academic theory. The homeless person as victim is at once both everywhere and nowhere, both visible and invisible. Victimisation of the homeless frequently takes place in full public view, yet because no-one really *sees* the homeless, because they appear only as shadows, this victimisation remains unacknowledged. It is easier to conceive of the homeless person as offender, the demon of the popular imagination and of political discourse. Equally, liberal and radical sensibilities may be attuned to the homeless as victims of social circumstance. What is noteworthy is the empty space into which the homeless person as victim of crime appears to fall, although, as will become clear, they are at a disproportionately high risk of such victimisation.

Victimology and homelessness

A brief chronology of studies of victimisation indicates that victimology was born in North America in the 1940s, parented by a positivist criminology and concerned to map the characteristics that defined and predicted victim status (Von Hentig 1948). Some welcomed this new focus on the victim as a corrective to the traditional criminological concern with the offender, while others have rejected it for its individualising and pathologising tendencies, with its theories of victim-proneness, victim-culpability and victim-precipitation.

In Britain, the 1970s saw the (re)discovery of the victim within academic circles, while across the Atlantic the victim movement gathered strength and focus (Sparks et al, 1977; Maguire and Pointing, 1988). Victimology remained significantly positivist in orientation with the development of new and more sophisticated - yet largely essentialist - models of victims and victimisation: perspectives such as the 'lifestyle-exposure' model retained a strong focus on the behaviour of the individual victim (Hindelang, Gottfredson and Garofalo, 1978).

It was not until the 1980s that more diverse perspectives began to develop in any significant fashion, although they had been in existence for some time before this: alongside a mainstream administrative victimology, feminist, left realist and critical perspectives began to emerge (Landau and Freeman-Lango, 1990; Walklate, 1995). The former maintained the positivist tradition within victimology in both theoretical and methodological approach, but, less obviously, positivist elements can also be detected within left realism, with its methodological commitment to surveys (albeit locally-based), in its empirical focus on victim 'lifestyle' factors, and in its pragmatic belief in the possibility of preventing crime, based on the identification of consistent and therefore predictable patterns of offender and victim behaviour. Furthermore, despite the radical theory and practice of feminist victimisation studies, there is an element of determinism in that the offender is constructed as active and male, and the victim as passive and female, in a way parallel to, though at the same time fundamentally different than, the early victimologists (Walklate, 1995).

Various dilemmas have presented themselves to the proponents of victimological perspectives: for the left realist, how to seek a pragmatic response to criminal victimisation without falling into the positivist trap; for feminists, how to document women's experience of violence without constructing or reinforcing notions of female passivity; and for victimology in general, perennial problems of definition and discourse. Critical victimology appears to offer us a way out from the first set of dilemmas yet, as I will argue later, faces a number of contradictions of its own. Informed by both left realism and feminism, critical victimology attempts to establish links between theoretical, empirical and political concerns. It also casts a critical eye on the development of victimology itself, questioning, for example, how some (mainstream, administrative) perspectives have become more influential than others (left realist, feminist) (Mawby and Walklate, 1994).

An unresolved issue for victimologists of all perspectives is that of discourse. Greater than a question of terminology or semantics is the debate concerning the ways in which we can talk about, and therefore conceive of, the processes of victimisation. The women's movement is often credited with the replacement of the term 'victim' with that of 'survivor', on the political grounds that 'survivor' connotes a sense of agency and empowerment, in contrast to the vulnerability and passivity implicit in 'victim' (Kirkwood, 1993). This discourse is now echoed by many new social movements, only some of which relate to criminal victimisation (Pitch, 1995).

Paradoxically, at the same time that those groups that have experienced acts legally defined, but not always socially recognised as, crimes have striven for recognition of their status as victims, there has been a widening (some would say devaluation) of the currency of the term. In the 1990s there has been a dangerous elision from the administrative criminological message that 'anyone can be a victim' to the profoundly reactionary 'we are all victims now': 'victims' of urban incivilities, various illnesses, the stresses of modern life, and of non-specific fears and unease. Newspaper headlines chosen almost at random at the time of writing include: 'Hamilton tells MPs he is "victim of injustice"' (*Guardian*, 18/7/97) and 'DSS victims left to "starve or

freeze'" (*Observer*, 20/7/97). As we approach the millennium we c
said to be in the era of the victim. Does such widespread use of th
of victimisation contribute to a recognition and correction of wron¿
it simply collapse disparate experiences into an undifferentὶ
ultimately meaningless category of 'victim'?

The academic consensus that the emergence of victimology siₗ
radical shift of focus from the criminal to the victim is challenged by rɪtch's
(1995) critique that the change was in fact one of semantics, not of
emphasis. That is, the discourse shifted from oppression to victimisation.
Within radical and critical criminology of the 1960s and 1970s, the criminal
was understood as an oppressed member of a class or collectivity, and crime
(of the streets) was theorised as the product of a divided, capitalist society
(Cohen, 1971; Hall et al, 1978). In a real sense, it was the 'criminals' who
were understood to be the 'victims'. of both social circumstance and of the
criminal justice system. Into the 1980s and 1990s the (apparent) shift of
focus from the criminal to the victim masks a fundamental change in
discourse, away from 'oppression' with its understanding of social dynamics,
towards 'victimisation' with its emphasis on internal, individual processes.

Victimological perspectives vary in the extent to which they claim an
ability to theorise the experiences of particular victim groups: the range is
from an administrative victimology with its relatively undifferentiated
'anyone can be a victim' philosophy, to critical and feminist victimologies
with their understanding of the uneven distribution of risks of victimisation
along gender and class faultlines. The case of the homeless victim
considered in this chapter challenges us to question the direction of the
criminological gaze which has largely been directed either towards the
homeless as victims of social circumstance, or towards homelessness as a
crimogenic phenomenon, but rarely at the homeless person as a victim of
crime.

There is a small but growing body of evidence which suggests that the
homeless are at disproportionate risk of crimes such as robbery, assault and
sexual violence (Snow and Anderson, 1983; Kelly, 1985; Daly, 1996), and
that there is a high level of victimisation prior to, but not necessarily
causative of, episodes of homelessness (Golden, 1992; Hendessi, 1992;
Kufeldt and Nimmo, 1987; Stein et al, 1994). This body of largely
sociological and social policy research has not been matched by detailed
victimological studies, despite the high levels of victimisation suffered by
this group of people. For such a tradition to develop, there would need to be
both a methodological and theoretical shift of focus.

At present the homeless are excluded equally from radical and official
surveys of criminal victimisation, so that a methodological shift would be
necessary to include those of 'no fixed abode' - a heavily victimised as well
as marginalised group - within national and local surveys. Theoretically,
constructs common to most victimologies - such as 'citizenship' - would also
undergo a transformation. Concepts of citizenship vary from conservative
criminology's emphasis on individual rights and citizenship to left realism's
vision of social rights and obligations, but none addresses the rights of those
not considered to be citizens at all (Corrigan, Jones and Young, 1989;
Mawby and Walklate, 1994).

The assertion that 'the status of autonomous political actor becomes derived from the recognition of one's common situation as victims' is persuasive in general terms but tells us little of those who are excluded from the body politic (Pitch, 1995:82). Victims in general and victim movements in particular may accept an identity constructed as passive, vulnerable and supplicant in exchange for political recognition and 'active citizenship', but this option is not usually open to victims who are also disenfranchised and (literally) dispossessed. The homeless are socially and economically as well as politically excluded from society: they do not (usually) vote, nor display much interest or trust in the mainstream political process, they have no fixed address (an important symbol of participation), and participate to only a limited extent in legitimate economic systems (Snow and Anderson, 1993; Carlen, 1996).

Homeless victims

The links between child abuse (both physical and sexual) and homelessness are well-established. Estimates vary, but a consensus is beginning to emerge that 40-50% of runaways and young homeless people (teenage to middle-20s) have been abused (Alder, 1991; Powers et al, 1990; Whitbeck and Simons, 1990; Hendessi, 1992; Stein et al, 1994). For those who are older (middle-20s onwards), domestic violence may precipitate episodes of homelessness (Golden, 1986). Following such primary victimisation often follows a second level, during which sanctions imposed by the State fall more heavily on the victim than on the perpetrator. Hagan and McCarthy (n.d.) refer to this process as 'double jeopardy' and the case of Leanne serves here as a useful illustration:

> My mum's husband was trying it on all the time and I didn't like it so I told her [mother] and she didn't believe me, then I got the authorities in about it, the social services, and she didn't like it because he got sent to prison about it ... First of all I moved in with my boyfriend and we broke up so I had to move out of there. I went to a friend's flat and that didn't work out, so I moved from there to my nana's house. Well from there I went to my mum's house, but I'm not supposed to be there because he's [stepfather] been charged with indecent assault. Well I had nowhere to stay, my mum kicked me out again, so the social worker fixed me up to stay here [YMCA hostel] (seventeen year-old white woman, Stoke-on-Trent).

Double jeopardy is a useful concept here, in both senses of the word: to be in danger of severe harm, and to be in danger resulting from trial for a criminal offence. Young victims of abuse can be forgiven for thinking that it is they who are on trial, given that removal from home and consequent loss of freedom is considered to be one of society's most severe sanctions (Parton, 1985). We can take this further still and argue that such individuals are subject to triple jeopardy in that, once removed to a care institution, accommodated in a hostel or living on the streets, they are subject to significant risk of further victimisation: harassment on the streets, bullying and robbery in hostels and institutional abuse and exploitation.

Katy was sexually abused by her stepfather and physically abused by her mother before leaving home aged sixteen. An ex-alcoholic (self- as well as officially-identified) with a history of involvement in public house brawls, at the time of interview she was aged nineteen and settled in a Birmingham hostel with her new baby. Contrary to the bluff 'you just get used to it' attitude of many homeless people, she expressed many generalised fears:

> I want shared or sheltered [accommodation] 'cause I'm used to being around a lot of people. I wouldn't like my own flat, 'cause even though I've got the baby I'd still be scared to be on my own ... I think the world's getting worse now [rather] than better ... the IRA will be over here soon. It gets me really paranoid sometimes to go out, just in case there's a man with a shotgun or something. It's really scary. If I'm walking down the street I think there's someone following me and I get really paranoid. Sometimes it stops me going out, I [have to] ask other people to go to the shops with me, 'cause I get really scared.

As a child, Katy had been prevented by her stepfather from leaving the house, and had been warned by him not to tell anyone about the abuse he perpetrated against her. In a real sense, then, the effects of the primary victimisation (child abuse) had transmuted into a secondary form, a generalised but intense fear of violence.

Designated, scapegoated and shadow victims

> ...victimization in general entails some kind of imposition of the death taint on the group that is victimized. They are one's designated victims. (Lifton, 1992:139).

Primary victimisation refers to the original event or process, such as being homeless (social victimisation) or being subjected to offending behaviour (criminal victimisation). Secondary victimisation connotes the suffering consequent on the primary process, and can be understood as a second or social death, the death of the person as a social being. Secondary victimisation arises from the discomfort, fascination, guilt and fear aroused by the visible suffering of the victim. Society can be said to feed psychologically from its designated victims, to regain its equilibrium via the processes of marginalisation and exclusion of the designated victim (Lifton, 1992).

Not all victims become designated victims, or scapegoats: a defining feature of those that do is their visibility, their obviousness as a source of discomfort and unease for mainstream citizens. A paradox of homelessness is that the street homeless in particular are both invisible and highly visible. They are visible in that they are constantly subjected to the media, political and academic gaze in their dual roles of civil and criminal offenders and social victims, and invisible or shadow-like in the general denial of their criminal victimisation and in the fact that no-one actually *looks* at the homeless, although they are seen to be everywhere (Sibley, 1995).

The scapegoated victim, like the homeless themselves, becomes a shadow, one that carries the death taint but does not literally die. The scapegoat by tradition is banished to the margins of society but is not extinguished, for they must continue to serve their function as 'sin-eaters' and as the recipients of displaced blame (Douglas, 1995). The concept of the invisible victim is well-established and is used to describe hidden, private and unreported crimes (Young, 1988). This goes some way towards explicating the victimisation of homeless people who experience crimes and incivilities that are often hidden from general view and remain overwhelmingly unreported. Such crimes and social harms, however, are often committed in public as well as private places, and are often simultaneously acknowledged and denied. 'Shadow victim' therefore is a more useful description of such victimisation, capturing the chiaroscuro nature of the process.

A street homeless person may be harassed, robbed or beaten, apparently in full public view, yet no-one will 'see' what happens:

> I mean you get the lager louts who go up to you and try to kick your head in. Then you get gangs of women walking around giving you lots of verbal abuse. I've been robbed a few times, yeah, mace sprayed on me once, somebody sprayed me with mace spray, took ten pound off me ... but it's mostly verbal abuse I get basically ... the last couple of days because of the heat I've been getting a lot more abuse, people tell me to eff off, you just gotta ignore it. But by the end of the day you're feeling pretty browned off, the fifteenth and twentieth time (Brendan, second-generation Irish man, *Big Issue* vendor and squatter in Manchester).

These routine activities on the city streets are constructed as trivial events, as incivilities rather than crimes, but continual abuse and harassment of the street homeless by the public is evidence of a process of scapegoating, of discharging tension and of displacing blame (Douglas, 1995). Perhaps the frustration with 'filthy beggars' that is commonly given verbal or physical expression on hot and dusty days in the city has its roots in a need to construct scapegoats.

For some, such a process is compounded by racist reactions to doubly marginalised, visible-yet-not-visible, black street people:

> You do get a little bit of trouble, selling the *[Big] Issue*, you get abuse 'cause you're homeless. At first it was a bit upsetting, but you just get used to it after a while ... It's not normally racist abuse, it's normally about being homeless, getting called scruffy and a tramp ... It can make it harder [being black], it can get a bit depressing, makes it seem worse. But I've learned to put it all behind me and just ignore it (Wesley, 24 years, self-defined as mixed race).

Wesley experienced racism as well as the general hostility directed at street people, and engaged in the familiar process of denial of harm which, as we shall see later, is one very important survival mechanism.

Brendan went on to observe that he was 'working his way up' by selling the *Big Issue* rather than begging, but that:

> .. since I've shaved off me beard, found a clean T-shirt and don't look so scruffy I've lost half me customers ... They think that to be homeless you've gotta go round in ten anoraks and a goatee beard, right?

In other words, he must look like a victim of circumstance in order to make a living on the streets, but if he does, he will be subject to abuse and harassment, and also be unlikely to have such victimisation acknowledged or legitimated. At the same time, the homeless are frequently shadow victims to themselves. At one level they deny or barely acknowledge the crimes committed against them, while at another the incidents and their consequences are recognised to have had a major impact on their lives. Such ambivalence is not unique to marginal groups, but is perhaps particularly marked among the homeless population, where the experience of crimes and incivilities is commonplace and where levels of reporting crimes to the police are exceptionally low.

There may also be complex psychological processes at work, wherein assumption of victim status or identity is not tenable when vulnerability to further victimisation is continued, and when the need to emphasise strength and survival is urgent. The complexity of this process is masked by the apparent simplicity of the common refrain 'you just get used to it'. To say that 'you get used to it' is to simultaneously recognise the fact of victimisation and to minimise its impact, in effect to normalise the crimes committed against them, to acknowledge their commonplace nature and the absence of any effective official response. There is, for example, no high-profile 'zero tolerance' policing strategy designed to tackle the crimes and incivilities suffered by the homeless.

Multiple, repeat and vengeful victims

Many respondents were multiple victims and had experienced some combination of child abuse, domestic violence, robberies, assaults, racist violence and 'social harms' such as verbal abuse and harassment (Genn, 1988; Hough, 1990; Aye Maung, 1995; Alder, 1991). Without subscribing to the positivist project of producing victim typologies and identifying regular patterns of victimisation, it is nevertheless true to say that such victimisation is not the outcome of a random process. Although there is no such thing as a 'typical' victim or victims, there are certain commonalities of experience, albeit mediated by structural factors of gender, age and ethnicity, as well as by personal biography. Young women aged 16 to 21, for example, had often become homeless following child abuse within the home, while those slightly older (21-plus) were likely (also) to have suffered violence within partnerships (Hendessi, 1992; Stein et al, 1994). Hostel-dwellers routinely experienced thefts and bullying, and the street homeless were frequently exposed to verbal abuse, threats and assaults (Golden, 1992; Snow and Anderson, 1993). Less well-documented is the level of sexual harassment and violence commonly directed at women and men, both in hostels and on the streets.

Two brief case-studies give some indication of the multiple victimisation commonly experienced:

> From the age of seven till I was fourteen I was sexually abused. So at the age of fourteen I left the house and was living on the streets for nearly two years, sleeping mostly under canal bridges, trees, benches, any place I could find ... He [stepfather] used to bring us [Sharon and her twin sister] out places and meet people and he even started us on porners [pornographic videos] ... Then at fourteen he got two guys to rape me ...

> Q. Have you been a victim of crime since you've been homeless?

> I've had many things done to me. I've had jewellery robbed, at least £400 worth of jewellery ... I've had a few beatings, I had one down in Moss Side. Not really serious bad beatings, just a few bruises on my back. Not really bad, bad beatings (Sharon, early 20s, Irish woman interviewed in a Manchester day centre).

And:

> The hostel is proper manic, it's evil believe me, you've got to have eyes in the back of your head, you've got to be tooled up, have CS gas or a blade with you, in case someone gives it to you ... because people get worried and they can't defend themselves ... I feel sorry for people like that 'cause I've been in hostels and geezers have got shagged up the arse ... I've actually seen it and heard it ... And in jail ... if you're in with the geezers you're ahead ... if you're not they're gonna batter you all the time, pick on you, attack you for your burn [tobacco] money, canteen money, batter you when you're in the exercise yard ... so it's hard and you've gotta look after yourself in this world (Tariq, aged 23, Iraqi/Scottish parentage, living in Birmingham).

Many of the homeless, therefore, are multiple victims, experiencing a wide range of crimes. They will also often be repeat victims, with crimes such as child abuse and harassment being, almost by definition, repeat offences. The breadth and depth of any individual's encounter with criminal victimisation, along with exposure to dangerous places (within the home and in institutions as well as on the streets), contributes to the normalisation of violence (Keane, 1996).

Such normalisation of crime is one reason for the massive under-reporting of crimes to the police. Other reasons include the denial of victim status, classification of incidents as non-crimes, feelings of guilt or unworthiness, lack of trust in the criminal justice system, difficulty in finding evidence and witnesses, and cultural constraints against 'grassing'.

Each of these is worthy of exploration in greater depth, but here I wish to consider just one factor in particular: the preference of 'vengeful victims' to deal (or at least be seen to deal) with incidents on an individual basis, rather than via the formal mechanisms of social control. Consider the testimony of Brian:

> I'd gone up to my room and the radio had gone. And I felt really embarrassed by it ... 'cause it was my incompetence for leaving the keys in the door ... 'cause it was my fault ... But yeah, something will be sorted out about it ... not in here ... not in this establishment. I'm too clever for that ... The staff have said to me that the police are very tired of coming out, but then again that's what they're paid for, so I don't see how they should be bored with it, really. Who else do you phone when you're a victim of crime? (second-generation Irish man, 19 years old, Manchester).

He did in fact contact the police, but was dissatisfied with their response, in particular the fact that they did not fingerprint his room: hence his resolve to 'sort it out' himself.

Kelly had been robbed while sleeping rough, and sought revenge on the perpetrators:

> I was sleeping rough on the Strand and met a couple of people, I got robbed ... I've been robbed but I haven't told anybody, you know what I mean? Just kept that quiet ... I've still got to sort out [the] people in London, 'cause they're the ones gonna get stabbed for robbing me in the first place ... that was my first lot of money, so people are sorting him out for me, but I want to go over and get the satisfaction myself, so I know it's done properly ... I only had a couple of pounds to last me a week and I was begging and begging for this money ... trying to sort my life out, sort out something to eat ... It's not right nicking off your own kind, [if] you nick off your own kind, you're nicking off everybody (white woman, early 20s, Birmingham).

Brian exhibited embarrassment and guilt in relation to having been robbed, which compounded the indications he received from hostel staff that there was little point in contacting the police. However, his threat to 'sort it out' may have been grounded more in the need to save face than in any real intention of confronting the suspected offender (Goffman, 1971). Kelly's indignation at having been robbed originated in the threat to survival presented by this loss of money, but also in the betrayal of trust that took place: 'I'd like to know why he done it ... he's hurt me 'cause he was a very, very good friend.' It is likely that there was more serious intent behind her threats to have him 'sorted out', not least because this was consistent with the code of honour expressed both within her family background, and by the marginal street culture to which she belonged.

Some important themes emerge here: the ways in which the victim becomes an offender (or at least a potential offender), not necessarily in any direct causal fashion, but as part of the web of risk and fear that characterises the lives of those who live at the margins. The impulse to 'sort things' for oneself is one important survival strategy in an indifferent or hostile environment, and this and other strategies for survival will be discussed below. First, let us consider the victimisation that takes place before a homeless career is begun.

Victims and survivors

Primary victimisation during homeless careers is as diverse as that experienced by the mainstream population, so in one sense general statements are neither possible nor useful. However, given the lack of research in this area, it is important to begin to document the victimisation of homeless youth, and to explore the inter-relationship between such victimisation and the development of their homeless careers. In doing so, themes of power and control begin to emerge: both victimisation as a form of control over the individual, and individual resistance strategies to such control.

The case of Katy illustrates the extent of control exercised over the victim both at the time of primary victimisation, and for a long while afterwards: her abuser in effect built prison walls around and inside her. Victimisation serves to control the homeless in a number of individual and communal ways. Crimes committed amongst the homeless population serve to generate mistrust, to maintain an individualised focus on self-preservation and to militate against the development of any sense of community (Snow and Anderson, 1993). Criminal acts by domiciled citizens against the homeless serve to spatially contain the homeless to (relatively less dangerous) ghetto areas, as well as to fulfil a scapegoating function (Davis, 1990; Douglas, 1995).

Brendan experienced the routine harassment meted out to the street homeless by 'respectable' citizens. He and many of his counterparts on the streets are society's designated victims, its scapegoats. The function of such violence - whether physical or verbal - is both to give expression to rage, hatred and fear, and to literally keep street people in their place. In order to survive, street people construct maps of 'safe' (that is, less dangerous) areas within the cityscape. The itinerant harassers serve as unorganised vigilantes keeping the city streets cleaned of deviant populations. It is not coincidental that relative safety should be sought by the homeless within marginal or deviant urban village areas. Brendan for example said that:

> At night I go to the Gay village 'cause there's a different style of people there, I mean people are a lot more caring ... they're not full of lager and ready for a fight.

Others sought safety in a community that spread across the city centre, rather than identifying particular places as their refuge. As we saw in chapter four, John said:

You hear about this streetwise stuff and it's not bull or nothing. It's a big bad jungle out there, man, and you gotta know where you're going and where you stand. I'd never get mugged, not me. 'Cause I know too many people, know all the people around town, so I'd never get mugged (21 year-old white man, on the streets of Manchester for five years).

He had nevertheless been threatened with a knife and chased when he went to the defence of a 'tramp' who had been verbally abused by some 'posh guy'. Still others attempted to avoid victimisation by seeking solitude:

It's just all the same. You get violence everywhere, wherever you go...I wouldn't mix with anybody, I'd just stay by myself ... There's nowhere safe on the streets ... Everyone thinks you're a down and out and that's it, but you're no down and out. You're a survivor (Andy, white man in his early 20s, on the streets for three years after leaving care).

His pessimistic (or realistic) assertion that 'there's nowhere safe on the streets' is counterbalanced by the rejection of the label of 'down and out' (social victim) and the positive claim of the identity of 'survivor'. This illustrates that the rejection of victim status is not necessarily rooted in a sense of unworthiness and illegitimacy, but may also have a positive dimension (Cretney and Davis, 1995).

At other times, avoidance strategies encompassed a sense of physical preparedness for trouble, a crisis-oriented management of personal space and a knowledge of dangerous people and dangerous places:

You know when something's gonna happen, the problem is if you're sat down you've got to try and stand up, but not run away unless you're sure you can get away. Just be ready to run as soon as you get the chance ... You know which ones are going to do it [threaten or use violence]. They're always the loudmouth group of lads ... the worst are the young people that go on the streets with loadsa money ... then they drink too much and don't know what they're doing ... [If] you go to the sort of proper drinking pubs and people come out of there, they'll throw you money (Ian, 25 year-old white man, based in Manchester).

Finally, humour is an important mechanism for dealing with the repeated incivilities that are not quite (but have the potential to be) criminal acts. Ian goes on to describe his strategy for diverting the hostile gaze:

It affects you at first then you just get used to people staring at you as you walk down the street ... [I just] give them a little wave. They get more embarrassed than you do.

Such embarrassment has a little to do with being caught in the act of staring, and a lot to do with the shocked realisation of the human agency of the deviant Other.

This set of avoidance strategies adopted by the homeless in relation to the threat of victimisation mirrors the avoidance and accommodation strategies

97

employed by citizens in their negotiation of city streets peopled by the 'new poor', including the street homeless (Taylor et al, 1996). In both cases, everyday routines are constructed to minimise interaction with the feared other, with the intention of minimising the risk of physical or social danger.

Alongside such avoidance strategies are a set of engagement mechanisms: proactive, often aggressive reactions to victimisation, to the threat of violence, or to a set of generalised fears. Such proactive engagement contributes to a breakdown in the distinction between victim and offender: individuals become offenders as well as (not *because of* as this is not an attempt at a causal explanation) being victims. Cases of violent engagement where individuals such as Kelly were motivated by revenge for their own victimisation have been discussed above, and appear straightforward enough. More disturbing for the liberal or radical conscience are those instances where the 'worthy victim' threatens to mutate into the street fighter, bully or homophobe.

Having experienced physical abuse at the hands of his father, Darren was acutely aware of his own potential for violence:

> I can't go back [home] 'cause if I go back I'll end up in hospital, 'cause me and my old man never got on ... So like last time I got kicked out because I had a go at him with an iron bar ... So if I go anywhere near the house I'll get beaten, I'll get literally put in hospital (18 year-old white man, Birmingham hostel).

After leaving home for the first time, Darren had served a four-month prison sentence for assault, and while in prison had witnessed bullying and had experienced violent 'welcoming committees' (Newton, 1994; Sim, 1994). Concerning the assault that led to his prison sentence:

> Well, the person was homosexual and he tried to get it on with me and ... I ain't fussed about homosexuals and all that lot if they keep themselves to themselves, but if they try to get it on with me, then it starts freaking me out and I got, I got a bit over the top and beat him up, and he took me to court for it.

There was nothing in his personal biography or wider cultural background to suggest that routine violence was not acceptable, nor that heterosexual masculinity need not be based on violent suppression of the Other.

No definitive conclusions are offered concerning the victimisation of homeless people: this is too under-developed an area to hope to do so on the basis of this ethnographic study. What is offered is an attempt to capture something of the complexities and ambiguities involved in the processes of victimisation. Chris is a case in point:

> [As a child] it was a case of 'shut up and do as you're told'. If you didn't shut up and do as you were told you'd get clobbered round the head all the time.

He left home at sixteen and later returned home:

But the relationship between me and my father just worsened again. When I, for the first time I can ever remember, spoke up for myself ... he lost his temper and he lashed out.

He left home again and went on to develop a relationship with a woman and to have a child. At the time of interview he was facing court proceedings, charged with physically abusing his daughter:

Her mother accused me of beating her up. Beating up my own child. She's done it before, it's been to court before. It was cleared then and put under NSPCC supervision. They were satisfied with the work that was done and so was I. It doesn't seem to have done the slightest bit good as far as her mother's attitude ... The condition on my bail sheet was that I didn't contact [his daughter] or her mother (White man aged 22, Manchester day centre).

Without proposing a simplistic 'cycle of violence' thesis, (and recognising that the charges against Chris had not been proven at the time of interview), nevertheless cases such as these challenge criminological theory to conceptualise some individuals as being simultaneously victim and offender. At present there is a polarisation between an understanding of the homeless as being either social victim or criminal, with little conceptual space for homeless people as the subjects of criminal victimisation. A shift of analytical focus would allow for their potential to be involved in varying levels of criminal activity, at the same time as being both social and criminal victims. Only then might they be understood, not as angels nor as devils, but as a complex and heterogenous group of people.

6 Regulating homeless spaces

The early 1990s was a period that saw an intensification of the trend towards the politicisation and criminalisation of street homelessness and its attendant 'symbols of incivility' (Hunter, 1985). Following the introduction of the Rough Sleepers' Initiative in 1990 it was asserted that no-one need any longer sleep rough on the streets of London, and in 1994 Prime Minister John Major declared that beggars were offensive 'eyesores' who needed to be removed from public view. In 1995 Shadow Home Secretary Jack Straw entered into the debate about street people when he expressed his concern about 'aggressive begging by squeegee merchants, winos and addicts' (*Guardian*, 9.9.95). This political debate conflated begging with both street homelessness and crime, thereby serving to demonise all street people. At the same time, the academic argument was developed that the incivilities of 'aggressive' begging and street disorder contribute not only to an increased fear of crime but lead also to an increase in crime itself (Kelling, 1995).

The urban-based ethnographic interviews cited in this chapter were conducted during the passage through Parliament of the Criminal Justice and Public Order Bill in 1993-94. The subsequent enactment of this legislation served to criminalise many activities and conditions associated with homelessness, such as travelling and squatting (Davis et al, 1994; Hawes and Perez, 1995). The early 1990s were also a time that saw the criminalisation of homelessness under old as well as new statutes. The number of arrests and prosecutions for begging increased fourfold in London: around 80% of those begging were estimated to be homeless (Murdoch, 1994). The vast majority of the beggars in this study (some 80%) had had some contact with the police while begging, 78% had been moved on, 67% had been cautioned, and 55% had been arrested, usually under the 1824 Vagrancy Act.

The moral climate of the time was such that ministers of religion as well as politicians exhorted the public not to donate money to beggars. This was an extraordinary, but certainly not unprecedented, Christian moral position (Christianity's moral ambiguity towards begging has been documented in chapters two and three). At the same time as this hardening of political, legal and moral positions was taking place, academic theorists of many disciplines were engaging in debates about the spatial and locational upheavals characteristic of the post-modern era. Dominant themes have been those of place and placelessness, of space and of shifting boundaries between spaces, of the search for identity and a disintegrating sense of private, communal and national 'home' (Shields, 1991; Bammer, 1992; Massey, 1992).

The discussion in this chapter of street homelessness as a socio-spatial phenomenon has been informed by theoretical debates concerning home and the city. First, there has been the tension between a generalised loss of a sense of home, alongside a significant increase in literal homelessness. Crucially, the street homeless have been constructed as dangerous precisely because there is no longer any clear or safe divide between the housed and the homeless. Economic and policy influences such as the 'right to buy' public housing, increasingly restricted definitions of statutory and involuntary homelessness, and an economic recession which has resulted in widespread negative equity among the property-owning middle-classes, have all served to alter communal notions of 'security' and 'home'.

Second, globalisation has created an urban culture that is characterised by fluid and shifting social and physical boundaries. Central activities relating to business, leisure and consumption are increasingly being removed from the urban core and relocated in peripheral shopping and leisure 'cities'. As these 'purified social spaces' are constructed, so the urban core increasingly becomes constructed as a site of danger and as a repository for urban fears and unease (Sibley, 1995). Attempts are made to redefine and make secure shifting boundaries, and above all to regulate those who inhabit the social margins of the city. The panopticon mall, for example, has become a geographically enclosed and socially secured space precisely because it has the means to exclude marginal street people (Davis, 1990).

The dangers represented by the homeless, along with attempts to make secure ever-changing social and geographical boundaries, result in what Sibley has described as 'geographies of exclusion' (1995). Minority groups such as the street homeless are dangerous precisely because of their marginality, their lack of a place or group membership. Mary Douglas tells us that 'all margins are dangerous ... Any structure of ideas is vulnerable at its margins' (1964:121). A clear separation of groups, therefore, is essential to the maintenance of purity and safety and the elimination of impurity and danger.

Spatial boundaries are used across cultures to assert a moral order (Duncan, 1983). In the post-modern and postindustrial city, spatial boundaries may not be as clearly delimited as in preindustrial societies, but they are no less rigorously enforced (Harvey, 1989). Indeed, the disintegration of known spatial arrangements may contribute to a greater felt need for clarity concerning such social constructs as 'place', 'home' and 'security'. There is something dangerously premodern about the poverty and apparent disarray of beggars and other street people that sits uncomfortably with the struggle for identity and a sense of place engaged in by the inhabitants of the post-modern city. The apparent order, conformity and stability of rural areas masks complex spatial dynamics and a rapidly changing socio-economic context. Far from representing the peaceful and functional *gemeinschaft* of the early theorists, there is in fact considerable

Figure 6.1 Panopticon mall: Arndale Centre, Manchester.
Photograph taken by the author.

potential for conflict and disruption within the countryside, as evidenced in recent times by the farming crisis, Countryside marches, and periodic moral panics about rural new age travellers (Sorokin and Zimmerman, 1929; Tönnies, 1955). Indeed, the deviant is arguably more conspicuous and therefore more likely to be subject to regulation when located outside of relatively anonymous urban spaces.

This chapter presents two extended case-studies of the regulation of homeless spaces and the marginalisation and exclusion of the homeless body. First, the case of homelessness in the counties of Gwynedd, Conwy and Shropshire provides a sense both of the nature of regulation and exclusion of deviance in rural areas, and of the strategies of resistance utilised by the rural homeless. The second case, that of Manchester's Cardboard city, examines the temporal and spatial aspects of the daily routines of street homeless people; begging and prostitution as subsistence or 'shadow work' activities; the spatial and social interactions of street people within marginal urban villages; and the nature of police regulation of deviant street life and networks.

Contested rural spaces

In recent years the rural has begun to be theorised as contested space, and the myth of the rural idyll in particular has been subjected to critical scrutiny (Philo, 1992; Cloke et al, 1997; Milbourne, 1997). Homelessness in rural areas is an especially contested phenomenon, at least partly because the homeless subject is especially visible and out of place within the pastoral landscape. Homeless people contravene both the indigenous rural moral order with its values of privacy and independence, and that of the incoming settlers with their expectations of scenery, security and escapism within an idealised countryside culture (Park, 1926; Duncan, 1983; Lawrence, 1995).

While it is true that the homeless are strikingly out of place in rural areas, it is also true to say that the homeless and the rural have both been constructed as representing natural rather than social space. Femaleness, the homeless, rural places and space itself have all been placed on one side of a binary divide, and have been identified with passivity, irrationality, nature and subjugation. These qualities have been couterposed against an active, masculine principle that is expressed through linear concepts of time, rationality and a hierarchical social structure (Massey, 1994). Both the homeless and the rural are therefore emblematic of chaotic nature, and understood as being in need of spatial ordering and regulation (Lawrence, 1995).

As we have seen in chapter two, historically the rural homeless have been constructed as the Other, as being ambiguously both an intimate part of rural society, yet somehow set apart. Such ambiguity is clearly to be found also in urban areas, yet the dangerous liminality of the homeless subject is amplified and compounded by the contradictions inherent in rural space. The rural has long been the repository of urban society's hopes and fears, with more recent myths of the rural idyll being superimposed on a much older contempt for an imagined dystopic and barbarian countryside (Mingay,

Figure 6.2 Myth of the rural idyll: a tourist view of North Wales.
Photograph taken by David Carter.

1989; Short, 1992; Bunce, 1994). Similarly, modern notions of the homeless as social victims form a thin veneer over more ancient constructions of the vagrant as both dangerous and disordered.

For marginal people occupying prime space, there are a range of risks and threats to their personal safety, well-being and sense of identity. Time spent being both visible and marginal within prime space is time spent assessing and managing risk. For those with spoiled identities such as the rural homeless, there is the constant task of negotiating a space within which they can maintain a degree of self-esteem, resisting an environment that offers significant assaults on the self (Goffman, 1959). Crimes against the person and onslaughts against a sense of identity are both highly personal and impersonal in their nature. That is, they are clearly experienced as personal attacks, yet they are targeted at an individual because of what, rather than who, they are. They may thus be understood as a form of punishment for the visible deviance presented by those who have 'homeless natures' (Foucault, 1980; Lawrence, 1995).

One form of assault on personal identity takes the form of contested claims, in which the individual's (albeit stigmatised) identity as a homeless person is challenged. Ellie had considerable insight into the complexities of presenting her persona to the public and recounted one illustrative story:

> When I was selling the *Big Issue* I had people coming up to me and saying 'you're not homeless', and I'm like 'are you judging me?' And it was just because I was looking clean. I'm not particularly clean at the moment, so now they accept that I'm homeless.

Jamie, a 31 year-old Scot, had been robbed while on the streets and assaulted on several occasions, and he understood that these were not purely random events. Rather, as he succinctly expressed it: 'I've been beaten up walking down the streets for being a tramp'. In his pragmatic way he accepted the spoiled identity of 'tramp' (along with the secondary identity of 'junkie'), and recognised the futility of seeking police intervention. His own moral code also restricted him from having recourse to the criminal justice system: 'I've been to prison and I wouldn't send anyone to prison, not unless it was a monster'. Symbolic assaults on the identity and physical assaults against the person are commonplace experiences among the homeless population, and may serve to deter all but the toughest or most desperate from visibly occupying prime spaces. Those who do remain visible are further subject to a range of formal and informal regulatory and exclusionary mechanisms.

Exclusion from the rural idyll

Homeless people are subject to individual assaults on their identity as well as physical attacks, both of which serve informally to spatially contain them: formal exclusionary and regulatory techniques are more usually directed at groups rather than at individuals. One of the most common, and certainly the simplest, forms of exclusion is the banning of unwanted populations from particular places. The summer of 1992 saw a series of moral panics throughout the nation concerning that modern folk devil figure, the new age traveller. Travelling youth were particularly attracted to rural and semi-rural areas and the atmosphere of moral panic in the county of Shropshire reached its height as the summer deepened. Traveller encampments were evicted from the deeply-rural border country, and travellers were effectively banned (by dint of regular police operations to move them on) from congregating in Mardol Head, one of the main squares in the tourist and market town of Shrewsbury (Carlen and Wardhaugh, 1992; Carlen, 1996).

Bangor, a student and cathedral city of some 17,000 people, is small and compact: with only one major shopping street, there are few places that marginal people can claim as their own. The only substantial shared public space outside of the shopping mall (which is out of bounds to street people) are the gardens around the cathedral. Marginal street people share this space with local residents, students and visitors, but for them it is their only venue for meeting with others, eating and drinking, carrying on their trades, and (often) sleeping at night. While interviewing Dill and Ellie in Cathedral Gardens, the police were questioning the street people sitting in the Gardens, and came close to making an arrest. Cathedral administrators had made complaints about the street people and wished to see them excluded from the Gardens, on the grounds of creating a public nuisance; they had also successfully requested that Thresher's (a wine shop) should ban them from their premises. Such spatial exclusions of marginal populations are hardly unusual, but have a particular impact in small towns serving rural areas, in that there is often, quite simply, nowhere else to go (see Davis (1990) for a classic analysis of the carceral city).

Furthermore, some street people are more spatially constrained than others: in theory at least, beggars who are not homeless can move on elsewhere, although there are often a limited number of towns and villages in which begging is possible. *Big Issue* vendors, in contrast, are only authorised to sell their product in specific locations. Dill, for example, was licensed to sell outside Thresher's, and although he was satisfied with the brisk business that went with this prime pitch in the middle of the High Street, he faced the dilemma that pursuing his trade not only brought him directly into the centre of contested space, but also required him to establish his pitch outside the same commercial premises from which he was banned. Thus, although he was participating in the legitimate economic practice of being a street vendor with a licence, he was nevertheless classified primarily as a homeless person.

Paradoxically, possession of a *Big Issue* badge does confer a legitimate economic status at the same time as it signifies homelessness and therefore a marginal social identity. As discussed further below, it is the visibility of street people that presents a direct challenge to the 'normal' use of prime space by 'respectable' citizens. The force of such a challenge is perhaps particularly evident within a rural context, given that the presence of street people conflicts with the image and myth of the rural idyll (Philo, 1992; Soja, 1997). Such myths are important in the marketing of areas such as North Wales as a tourist destination, but they serve also to obscure the economically underdeveloped nature of the region (Cloke et al, 1997).

Exclusionary efforts are not confined to town centres and deeply-rural areas, but may also occur within residential neighbourhoods: indeed the

Figure 6.3 Geographies of exclusion: Cathedral Gardens, Bangor.
Photograph taken by the author.

phenomenon popularly known as 'nimbyism' is perhaps one of the best known spatial regulatory techniques. One instance of this took place in Shropshire in 1992, a period not at all coincidentally when anti-traveller rhetoric was at its height. The vilification was such that even sympathetic voluntary sector workers were moved to dissociate themselves from the travellers, defining them as not really homeless and in danger of 'getting the homeless a bad name'. Within the context of such discourse, the following episode took place:

> The government's plan to build a network of bail hostels [which take homeless offenders who otherwise go to prison] ... is in danger of being thwarted ... by local communities whose reaction to a proposed development is 'NOT in my backyard' ... Plans for a 27-bed unit in Shrewsbury were scotched earlier this year when 18 families in the Belle Vue neighbourhood stumped up more than £200,000 to buy the proposed site. Derek Conway, Conservative MP for Shrewsbury and Atcham, who helped the campaign against the Shrewsbury scheme, said: 'I think Nimbyism is wholly defensible' (*Guardian*, 20/7/92).

Exclusionary tactics, then, are frequently directed at those with homeless natures: those who are visibly homeless or are travellers, and therefore unwelcome within prime rural space. Other efforts to exclude are directed at the symbols of incivility associated with homelessness, in particular begging and sleeping rough (Hunter, 1985). For example:

> I've been charged for begging, went to court, they gave me a conditional discharge and I wasn't allowed in that town again. It was a place ... in the Forest of Dean (Dill).

Such moving-on of troublesome populations is an ancient response, one that has been an established feature of the itinerant life for centuries (Beier, 1985). At one level it may be experienced as a 'softer' punishment than other criminal justice sanctions, while at another level it constitutes a sustained attack on a sense of self, serving both to construct and to reinforce stigmatised identities. Jamie tells his story:

> I was camping up at Balloch, at Loch Lomond ... and they came out with some crappy new laws in Scotland about Loch Lomond, so the polis is always around hassling you, chasing you, and the park rangers and all that, telling you to get out ... So if I'm sleeping out somewhere it's 'C'mere you, you're done for a breach', so I'm never out of jail up there, I'm always being jailed, just for being there.

Many street homeless people survive in the larger towns and cities by occupying marginal or interstitial places within general prime space: in smaller towns and villages, however, there are insufficient hidden or marginal places into which deviant or stigmatised populations can disappear.

Rural space is highly-regulated, with apparently open and wild vistas in fact encompassing a tight series of privately-owned spaces. Social and physical survival for marginal populations often depends on their ability to identify and make use of any liminal places that may exist within this socio-spatial order. Rural homeless people should not be understood as passive targets of exclusionary and regulatory techniques: rather, many of them engage in their own strategies of resistance. Such strategies fall into the two broad categories of *identity work* and *negotiation of space*. Ellie, for example, had developed a sophisticated range of resistance strategies, one of which centred around a careful presentation of self, and another which involved seeking refuge in the open roads (Goffman, 1959). In the latter respect, Ellie never stayed in one place for longer than a few weeks at a time, but used Bangor as her home base and adopted an intermittent travelling lifestyle: 'I make myself a destination and then I just go in that direction and stop in towns along the way'. During her settled periods, she drew on the resources deriving from her middle-class background in order to present an image of self that she believed would be congenial to figures of authority:

> I was arrested for begging ... [but] I'm lucky because I've figured it all out, I'm very good at blagging 'cause I've got a posh accent ... What's worked best is being polite, when I got arrested and taken to Caernarfon [police station] all I got was an informal warning, and they even gave me a lift back to Bangor (laughs). I was making friends with them, you've just got to pretend to be polite.

For others, their techniques can be characterised as a survivalist 'beg, steal or borrow' philosophy, tempered by an 'honour among thieves' ethos:

> Before selling the [*Big*] *Issue* I begged, borrowed, I stole. I'm not a major criminal or nothing, the stuff I steal is petty, and I never steal off my own kind ... I'm just a petty thief. I don't go out to steal or to cause anyone any harm.

Jamie's economic strategies for survival were accompanied by a substantial amount of identity work: he was prepared to accept the spoiled identities of 'tramp' and 'junkie', but rejected the label of 'major criminal' in favour of that of the 'petty thief' who causes little harm and who refuses to steal from his 'own kind'.

In order to survive, street homeless people need to have a highly-developed sense of place. Their mental maps operate on a number of different levels, from their detailed local knowledge of how towns and villages are structured both socially and spatially, to a sense of the nature of other rural and urban places. None of the North Walian interviewees had been born in the region, and all had attachments - both actual and idealised - to other places. They all had the option of living elsewhere and to varying degrees had chosen to live in their present locations, whether for positive ('it's quieter here') or for negative ('it's worse elsewhere') reasons. For some, there was evidence that they themselves had been influenced by the myth of the rural idyll, in that they felt themselves to be escaping from an urban nightmare:

> I don't like the cities 'cause I get a load of shit, 'specially being on the streets. It's quieter here, you've got homeless people in the town [Bangor], but you haven't got any badheads. Not like in Piccadilly ... I was getting loads of hassle when I was in Manchester, and so I thought 'Bangor, a small town, somewhere quiet by the sea' (Dill).

For others, however, the rural idyll was complicated by questions of national identity, language and a sense of belonging (Ching and Creed, 1997). Not having been born in Wales, they needed to negotiate their way around the countryside in an attempt to find a space for themselves. They frequently felt most 'at home' in Bangor, a student town with a large youth population, but were rather more uncomfortable ten miles away in Caernarfon:

> I come to Bangor most of the time ... you can do Caernarfon, but everyone's very Welsh in Caernarfon, so it's a bit dodgy if you're English and you're playing Irish tunes, 'cause you might get someone coming along and beating you up (Ellie).

Time and space on the streets

Homelessness is above all a spatial phenomenon. To be homeless is by definition to be a person without a place of one's own, to be someone who is dis-placed or out-of-place. Traditional theories of space, however, prove less than useful in analysing the use of space by street homeless people. The classic division of space into public and private domains has been oriented towards the explication of the use of space by the domiciled population. 'Public' and 'private' are meaningful terms when there is a public and potentially dangerous region to venture into from the safe, privatised domain of the home. For the street homeless, however, the public-private dichotomy has far less relevance. For them, the distinction between public and private is less clear-cut in that they are routinely excluded from many public, as well as most or all private, places. Furthermore, their survival strategies frequently involve them in attempts to privatise public space: for example, to at least temporarily claim a public place such as a shop doorway for their own private usage.

An alternative distinction between prime and marginal space is more relevant to an analysis of the street homeless population, whose major concern is not with the public or private nature of properties, nor even with the question of ownership (Duncan, 1983; Snow and Anderson, 1993). Rather, their concern is with the value which settled communities ascribe to particular places. Prime spaces are those that are of residential, commercial,

Figure 6.4 Piccadilly Gardens, Manchester: a place for recreation.
Photograph taken by Chris Carter.

recreational or other use to settled citizens, or else those that have symbolic value to them in that they represent order and civility (Hunter, 1985).

Marginal spaces have long been ceded to the homeless, or even allocated to them willingly, in order to confine them to, and contain them within, Skid row or Cardboard city areas of cities and towns (Spradley, 1970; Hope and Young, 1986; Glasser, 1988; Hoch and Slayton, 1992). Importantly, these designations are not static: marginal land may, for example, become prime space under the transforming process of gentrification, and it is within such a context that struggles over the use and ownership of space must be understood (Abu-Lughod, 1994).

Homelessness is perceived as dangerous because, and arguably only if, it is visible in public places, and it is this visibility that represents a threat to the secure sense of place enjoyed by settled citizens. Thus, it is not marginality in and of itself that is so dangerous, but rather the visible presence of marginal people within prime space that represents a threat to a sense of public order and orderliness. The dilemma for the street homeless population is that the exigencies of daily subsistence require that they frequently enter prime space, and so face potential conflict with settled citizens concerning the use of space. This was particularly the case in Snow and Anderson's (1993) study of Austin, Texas, where the dispersal of facilities for the homeless over a wide geographic area entailed their repeated entry into prime urban space. In contrast, Manchester's homelessness circuit (voluntary and charitable provision of subsistence facilities) is located within an area of around one square mile, situated between the city's two mainline railway stations and alongside its main shopping, business and leisure districts.

The location of this homelessness circuit within the city centre seems not to be consonant with the argument that the homeless are not welcome, nor indeed even tolerated, within prime urban space. During fieldwork, however, it emerged that venues on the homelessness circuit were invariably located in interstitial or marginal places within prime city centre space. Thus, day centres were usually situated in back alleys or other inconspicuous locations. Furthermore, if prime space was to be used, then this would take place predominantly at marginal times of the day, outside main business and shopping hours. The prime site of Piccadilly Gardens, for example, would often be avoided by the street homeless during the day for fear of being moved on by the police. However, it could be used by voluntary agencies for the distribution of food and clothes in the evenings, once shoppers and workers had returned home.

Time, then, as well as space, begins to emerge as a significant dimension to the social ordering of the homelessness circuit. Although it is reasonable to argue that 'over time, spatial practices, the habitual routines of space ballets are concretised in the built environment and sedimented in the landscape' (Shields, 1991:53), it is also true that the social meanings (and therefore appropriate usage) of particular places are not fixed for all time but are subject to shifts and changes. Such changes in meaning and usage may take place over years or months, but may equally well occur on a daily basis. Piccadilly Gardens is a case in point. The Gardens serve a number of functions, accommodating shoppers, tourists and office-workers during

Figure 6.5 Piccadilly Gardens, Manchester: a place under surveillance.
Photograph taken by Chris Carter.

'respectable' daylight hours, after which they are used as an outdoor soup-kitchen in the evenings, before again becoming a no-go area for street homeless people during the hours of night-time and early morning. Regular police patrols during these hours serve to keep this area free from rough sleepers and thereby safe for domiciled citizens at leisure in the neighbouring pubs, clubs and restaurants.

Giddens says that 'co-ordination across time is the basis of the control of space' (1990:18), and the following account of daily subsistence on the homelessness circuit illustrates both the temporal and spatial nature of this ordering of daily routines:

> Well, I'd have to move anytime from eight o'clock onwards when the shops start to open, and then I go to the Salvation Army for my breakfast and a dinner. From 10 o'clock in a morning, till three o'clock anyone is welcome to have a free breakfast, free dinner. Then I go to St. Augustine's Church, it's a Catholic Church in Oxford Road, get a butty, a brew there, then that takes us up to about four o'clock. Then we go Chinatown, have a few hours there. Then the handouts [in Piccadilly Gardens] come out about now, between nine and half past....

> Lifeshare, they are round every night, they come and bring condoms, needles, tea for the girls on the red-light district. For homeless people, at half past nine they bring blankets, hot pies, soup. But ... I just generally walk around the streets. There is places to go, but it's generally day centres for starters. There is a day centre in Salford and there is one opened up in Stockport. It's just generally day centres we have to be in like, so as not to be on the streets, people just don't want you on the streets.

> We just move amongst ourselves, and make us own entertainment. Like we'd probably go to a night club, or probably have a night playing cards, rather than meeting in an alleyway, and that's our entertainment. Because after say six o'clock or seven o'clock, that's the last day centre I know that shuts at seven at night, that's Salford Cathedral. The day centre shuts at seven. But ... from seven onwards [you've] just got to be on the street and just lie low, and if you don't know where the handouts are you have just got to find them. But I'd generally be in Piccadilly Gardens and in Chinatown. If you're round there anytime from nine o'clock onwards, you can always find out where they [street homeless people] are (Pete, white man aged 25).

Life on the streets is extremely time-consuming, with the simplest of subsistence and personal maintenance tasks requiring the expenditure of much time and effort (Russell, 1991; Snow and Anderson, 1993). Furthermore, time is qualitatively as well as quantitatively different for street people, in that it takes on a cyclical rather than linear quality. Time on the streets is cyclical partly because there is little in the way of future

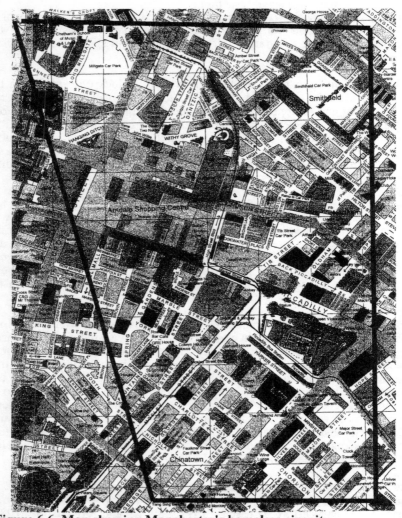

Figure 6.6 Map showing Manchester's homeless circuit.
Based upon the 1998 Manchester City Centre (1:3,500) Ordnance Survey
map, by permission of Ordnance Survey on behalf of the Controller of Her
Majesty's Stationery Office © Crown Copyright MC100029383.

orientation, life being dominated by the urgency of daily subsistence needs, and partly because the agencies on the homelessness circuit are also locked into a cycle of daily survival (Murray, 1986).

The repetitive, present-oriented and often tedious nature of time on the streets is reminiscent of prisoners' accounts of 'doing time' (Cohen and Taylor, 1972). Indeed the analogy between doing time on the streets and in prison is not a new one, but was made almost thirty years ago by James Spradley (1970), with his description of men on Skid Row doing 'life-sentences on the installment plan'. An interesting comparison elsewhere within the criminal justice system may be made between police officers and street homeless people. One police inspector involved in the research observed that both groups were adept at locating resources that may ameliorate conditions on the city streets:

> You hear it said that a policeman never gets wet and he never gets cold. In fact we've got a lot in common with the homeless, we're the only ones out on the streets all night and we know how to stay warm (laughs). Not many people know about the warm-air ducts outside restaurants, for example.

However, police officers are only on the streets for fixed periods and have homes to return to, so we should not be tempted to take this analogy too far. Most important, they have an established place on the city streets. Homeless people have no legitimate identity while on the streets, and continually face the problem of how to negotiate their potentially dangerous status. The spatial ordering of their lives on the homelessness circuit goes some way towards reducing the unease caused by their marginal subsistence. However, this spatial ordering must be repeatedly carried out over time if this deviant population is to be (seen to be) adequately contained and controlled.

The perceived need for this spatio-temporal ordering arises from the liminal status of street homeless people within urban society. Liminality describes a state of being in-between, within which individuals are in transition between various positions in society, or between particular stages in the life-course (Van Gennep, 1960; Turner, 1974, 1979; Shields, 1991). Unlike 'marginality', 'liminality' captures more fully a sense of process, of becoming, of events unfolding over a period of time. Thus, someone does not simply become deviant or marginal at a fixed moment in time, but rather continuously engages in the process of becoming and being deviant.

Homeless people are perpetually in a state of transition and homelessness itself is not a fixed state. Someone may typically sleep rough for a period before finding hostel accommodation, or may squat an empty property for a while before sleeping rough. Furthermore, whether sleeping in or out of doors, homeless people are likely to have a wide spatial range. In particular, they become highly visible as they move between prime and marginal spaces, and thus become perceived as potentially disordered and dangerous. Theirs is a liminal existence, positioned as they are somewhere between the highly-ordered urban worlds of business, residence and leisure.

Paradoxically, while the inhabitants of these ordered worlds fear and distrust the street homeless, they may also romanticise the nature of their existence: their marginality is threatening, but it may also be appealing. There is a common belief that, despite the physical privations and dangers, there is an existential freedom to be found on the streets (Andersen, 1923; Bruns, 1980; Orwell, 1933). As we have seen this is not so. Life on the streets is not exciting, unorganised and spontaneous, but rather tedious, predictable and closely regulated. Ordered and orderly, a large part of the daily life of street homeless people is spent pursuing the means of subsistence, and it is to the nature of these survival strategies that we now turn.

Living in Chinatown

For those people unable or unwilling to wholly subsist on the legitimate homelessness circuit, there exists the option of engaging in a range of illegitimate or quasi-legitimate survival strategies within Cardboard city. Cardboard city is not an urban village in the sense of a fixed community consisting of an established area of residence and an identifiable population with specific cultural or subcultural characteristics, values and identities. Nor yet is it simply an urban jungle, characterised as 'transient, depressed if not brutal...[a] Skid Row, Tenderloin [or] red-light district' (Gans, 1962:4).

Cardboard city may at times appear to be an urban village in its identifiable membership and sense of community, and at others an urban jungle in its disorderliness, impoverishment and lawbreaking activities. However, Cardboard city cannot simply be understood either as Gans' ideal-typical urban village or urban jungle. Cardboard city is, by definition, a region of shifting locations, populations and identities. Above all it does not exist as a separate entity within the ecology of the city. It is essentially dynamic and interactive, and its citizens definable in relation to other urban locations and populations. For it is the boundaries between areas, both symbolic and physical, which allow for a clearer understanding of the role and function of each area. Furthermore, it is the maintenance or transgression of these boundaries that is central to this analysis of the interaction between Cardboard city and its neighbouring areas.

This formulation contrasts with more static ecological explanations, which conceive of deviant areas and deviant street populations as being discrete and self-contained. In his study of New York City, Cohen (1980) argues that different deviant groups remain geographically separate, with female prostitutes and street homeless men rarely intruding into the other's territory. In Manchester, by way of contrast, Cardboard citizens and other marginal groups such as sex trade workers entered into complex negotiations concerning the use of space, both with each other and with their domiciled neighbours. A case in point is the overlapping spatial boundaries of Cardboard city and the red-light district: homeless people and prostitute women shared a particular daycentre, separated only by time, with homeless street people using the centre by day and sex trade workers claiming the night hours (see chapter one for a discussion of fieldwork in this location).

Within the 'world of strangers' that constitutes urban life, street homeless people can be understood as 'unpredictable strangers' (Lofland, 1973; Snow and Anderson, 1993). Existing on the margins of legitimate social worlds, they evoke ambivalent responses of fear and pity. They are perceived as both needy and dangerous, at once the victim and the victimiser. Street homeless people must take cognisance of these responses and perceptions in their attempts to seek minimal shelter and the means of subsistence.

Living and sleeping rough on the streets is both highly transgressive and highly vulnerable. Vulnerable because the defensive guard essential to all urban dwellers (and especially those whose 'home' is on the streets) must be lowered once asleep. Street homeless women, in particular, are vulnerable to sexual assault and harassment, while both women and men routinely experience physical assault and verbal abuse (the victimisation of homeless people was discussed at length in chapter five; see Alder, 1991; Hendessi, 1992; Douglas and Gilroy, 1994). Sleeping and living rough is transgressive because the functions and routines of daily life are translated from the private domain of the home to the public space of the streets. Routines which are experienced as safe and domestic when conducted in private become dangerous and polluting when exposed to public view. Danger is not inherent in the activities of eating, sleeping, urinating or washing, but arises from the moral ambiguity created by such activities occurring in the wrong place.

In this way, street homeless people and their paraphernalia of subsistence become 'matter out of place' (Douglas, 1964). Their daily routines and personal functions are perceived as both literally and symbolically polluting. This association between street people and dirt is often to be found in both popular and criminal justice discourses. Beggars are described by politicians and the media as 'dirty', 'offensive' and 'eyesores', while the police mount periodic 'sweeps', in a bid to 'clear' the city streets of beggars.

Street homeless people may negotiate this transgressiveness and vulnerability by attempting to neutralise their perceived dangerousness and mask their neediness, and they often achieve this by privatising public space (Lofland, 1973). It has long been recognised that certain groups of people attempt to claim specific areas of the city as their own: for example, youth gangs fighting over their 'turf', office workers claiming part of public parks as theirs, or indeed street homeless people habitually occupying 'their' park bench. Lofland's (1973) observations on the locational transformations effected by such attempts at creating 'home territories' were made primarily in relation to the domiciled urban population: for those with little or no control over private places and with limited legitimate access to public spaces, the need to privatise public space is at once more urgent and more difficult to satisfy.

Okely notes in her illuminating study of spatial ordering and symbolic boundaries in relation to the inside-outside dichotomy so vital to traveller-gypsy culture that:

The area of order [inside the trailer] is extended by laying pieces of carpet or new linoleum immediately outside the trailer (1983:86).

119

Without suggesting that street homeless people may be understood as an ethnic group comparable to traveller-gypsies, nevertheless the negotiation of space involved in the arrangement of blankets and cardboard on city streets is more than a random and purely physical activity. There is also a significant social dimension in that an individual's sleeping equipment is carefully placed so that it becomes a marker and a symbol of their territory, however temporary that may be. Just as with the Traveller-Gypsies, such territorial claims are likely to be disputed, and thus to bring them into conflict with the settled community. Rarely, however, are territorial claims abandoned under such pressure. In the interests of a measure of physical and psychological safety, such conflicts over the use of space must repeatedly be negotiated. In particular, some public space must be claimed for private usage. The degree of success of this privatisation of public space may vary widely, from a blanket placed in highly vulnerable locations such as shop doorways, to relatively safe, semi-private shelters in Chinatown.

Terry, a white man aged twenty, gives an account of his successful attempt to privatise some public, albeit marginal, space for the private function of sleeping:

> [We've been] sleeping down in Chinatown, down a back alley in this shelter, under this set of stairs. It like had a cage round it and a door on the front of the cage, and we got blankets and put them all up [with] cardboard on the outside and cardboard on the floors and blankets on the floors, so it was quite warm. It was roughing it but it wasn't rough roughing it, if you know what I mean. [We were] kipping out in the open but it was sheltered. There's quite a few places like that around town, where you can get your head down.

Shadow work

Shadow work may be defined as those subsistence activities engaged in by the homeless which are outside of the regular employment system, but not necessarily outside of the market system altogether (Illich, 1981; Snow and Anderson, 1993). Street homeless people are on the whole excluded from legitimate labour exchange, and must therefore participate within a shadow labour market. State benefits are technically available, but difficult to obtain under the conditions prevailing on the streets: few if any of those interviewed during fieldwork reported receiving full benefits payments.

Agencies on the homelessness circuit go some way towards meeting subsistence needs not satisfied by the benefits system, and Chinatown businesses provide food and basic shelter for some (but by no means all) rough sleepers. However, the homelessness circuit and Chinatown cannot meet all the subsistence needs of everyone living in Cardboard city. In particular, they cannot provide money, at least some of which is essential to all those living, however tenuously, within a cash economy. Street homeless people, therefore, are likely to have to engage at some point in shadow work. This may not be work as traditionally conceived, with contracts, regular hours and pensions, but is nevertheless work in the sense that time and effort are expended in return for money, goods or services. Shadow work does not

120

Figure 6.7 Shadow work: *Big Issue* vendor, North Wales.
Photograph taken by the author.

often follow highly regulated routines, but is nevertheless structured as to time and place.

It is certainly meaningful to refer to street homeless people 'going to work', in the sense that they engage in regular activities which earn them sufficient to meet their daily subsistence needs. Such activities may be legitimate (such as selling the *Big Issue*), illegitimate (services associated with prostitution), or quasi-legitimate (begging). Interestingly, the degree of legitimacy of a particular form of shadow work is not necessarily closely related to its degree of acceptability to the settled community. Legitimate sellers of the *Big Issue*, as well as beggars and prostitutes, report harassment by the public and injunctions to move on by the police.

Begging is the shadow work activity most closely associated with street homelessness, although in recent years *Big Issue* vendors have become a significant presence on some city streets, clearly identifiable as homeless (although not necessarily street homeless) people. Begging appears to the public view as a random and uncoordinated, and therefore potentially threatening and dangerous, activity. It is, in fact, subject to systematic temporal and spatial ordering. Begging in Manchester takes place at specific times and in particular places. Perhaps unsurprisingly, the main area for begging is the main shopping district, a district that incorporates the busiest pedestrian thoroughfares of the city. An important exception is the covered Arndale shopping mall, which is effectively a no-go area for beggars. Regular private security patrols are highly effective in clearing these 'streets' of beggars, significantly more so than police efforts with regard to open-air shopping streets. In this respect, as in many others, such malls represent a purified social space (Sibley, 1995).

Begging, unlike other subsistence activities associated with living and sleeping rough, seldom took place in Chinatown. Fieldwork in this area suggested that this resulted from a tacit agreement between street homeless and business people concerning spatial arrangements. The understanding was that food, water and sleeping spaces would willingly be provided, if the street homeless presence was confined to marginal back alley-ways, rather than being in evidence at the frontages of the shops and restaurants that constitute the prime space of Chinatown.

Homeless people begging had motivations that ranged from acquiring just enough money to meet that day's food and shelter needs, to supporting a drug habit. As with any other form of work, shadow workers had a clear idea of how much money they needed (or were able) to earn each day. For one drug-user:

> If it's just to make you feel better, [you would need] about ten or twenty pound, know what I mean, just to get by. But like if you were doing it to get the hit, it would mean more like forty, fifty pound a day, maybe sixty pound a day (Ricky, white man aged 25).

Others compared likely monetary gains to be made from (quasi-legitimate) begging with the (legitimate) selling of the *Big Issue* and concluded that they preferred the safer activity of vending, albeit with its lower returns, rather than the risks associated with begging or other quasi-legitimate or illegitimate activities:

> So usually [when I finish selling] I've made my money for the next day's *Issues*. Like I'll blow all my money today and tonight ... [and keep] three pound or six pound to get ten or twenty *Issues* tomorrow, and I'll be sound then. That will help me through the day then. It's a lot easier than shoplifting or begging, isn't it? (Jimmy, white man aged 24).

A comment by Kaz illustrates homeless people's awareness of the political issues surrounding their use of prime space, and the implications that conflicts over the use of space are likely to have for their subsistence strategies:

> They're trying to recreate the city centre aren't they [and it] don't help them much me hanging round selling the *Issues*. I can't see what problem it makes though. I could be a *Manchester Evening News* vendor, couldn't I? It's all right for buskers, you know it probably makes the place look dainty or something, having buskers round, something for the tourists to look at.

The lady is a tramp?

> ... it almost seems as though to be a woman - an individual, not part of a family or kin group - in the city, is to become a prostitute - a public woman (Wilson, 1991:8).

If it is true that for *any* woman to be alone in the city is (almost) to become a public woman, a woman of the streets, then how are homeless and placeless women constructed? A male tramp is one who is out of place because he is homeless and destitute, while the female tramp is the sexual delinquent and the unaccommodated woman. If male tramps evoke fear and pity, then female tramps arouse hatred and desire. The beggar is an uncomfortable reminder of poverty amid relative affluence, while the female prostitute is the universal and reviled symbol of dangerous yet enticing heterosexualities. The liminality of both groups lies partly in the ambivalence of response that they evoke in respectable citizens, and partly in their diurnal shifting between prime and marginal spaces.

Street prostitute women relate to their environment in a way that is succinctly expressed by the phrase 'on the beat'. Women on the beat engage directly with the city streets in search of business, in contrast to their higher-status sisters who work indoors (Hoigard and Finstad, 1992). Women on the beat are both at home on the city streets (precisely because they work these streets), and endangered by life on those same streets. In Manchester, the main area for female street prostitution is the red-light district bounded by Minshull, Sackville and Chorlton streets. This district is adjacent to the Gay village that centres on Bloom and Canal streets, and close to Chinatown, whose boundaries are Portland, Mosley, Princess and Charlotte streets. The red-light district also overlaps to a certain extent with Cardboard city

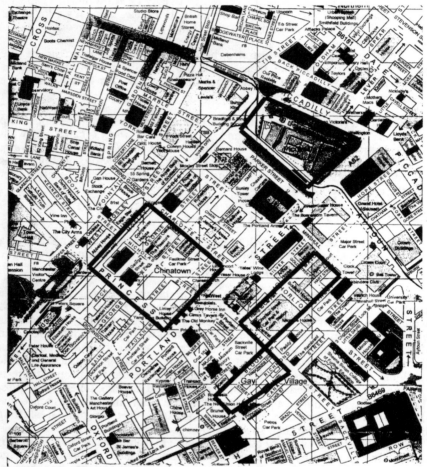

Figure 6.8 Map showing key areas within Manchester city centre: (clockwise from top), Piccadilly Gardens, Chorlton Street red-light district, Gay village and Chinatown.

Based upon the 1998 Manchester City Centre (1:3,500) Ordnance Survey map, by permission of Ordnance Survey on behalf of the Controller of Her Majesty's Stationery Office © Crown Copyright MC 100029383.

(although the latter has wider and more fluid boundaries) and contains within its borders some key venues on the homelessness circuit. One venue in particular was used as a drop-in centre for the homeless during the day, and as a resource centre for prostitute women at night (see also chapter one).

These areas or villages may be physically mapped, a process that relies on the collation of a series of individual mental maps (Pocock and Hudson, 1978; Gould and White, 1974). Both agency staff and street homeless people gave accounts of the mental maps that they used in negotiating their daily lives within city spaces. Street people used these cognitive maps both to orient themselves towards their environment, and as a basis on which to minimise risk within their daily routines. Clearly, such spatial ordering is not confined to street people, but does take on a particular immediacy and urgency for those whose entire existence is conducted on the streets.

Terry had a clear mental map of the urban villages relevant to his subsistence on the streets, while Dave's mapping shows the ways in which daily choices concerning mobility and safety may be made:

> It's like the beat, it's Sackville Street, Minshull Street and all that. And there's Piccadilly ... Piccadilly's for the mostly homeless people. Chorlton Street's for the rent boys, prostitutes and queer....sorry, gay community (Terry).

> Well ... there's only like the red-light district where I won't go, and that's only a few streets like, around Chorlton Street bus station area. But apart from that I'll go anywhere, I just keep out of the way in that area, and that's only at night-time. Once it goes dark it's only rough then, I mean you can walk round in the day and have no trouble, it's just the times when the prostitutes are out and everything, when it's a bit rough to walk around then (Dave).

Other street homeless men disagreed on these questions of time and place, and believed the red-light district to be 'wild' by both day and night, and therefore to be avoided whenever possible.

What then of the women who work these streets? Not all were homeless, but both agency staff and the women themselves suggested that there was a strong link between homelessness and prostitution. This link was likely to be one of two types: either women entered prostitution for economic reasons and subsequently found themselves to be homeless or badly-housed because of their chaotic lifestyle; or else they were young homeless women who became engaged in exchanging sexual services for money or shelter, once they found themselves on the streets. National and international studies have found the latter phenomenon to be a common one with, for example, one study finding that one in seven homeless young people had exchanged sex for money (Centrepoint, 1995).

Ethnographic data illustrates the nature of economic links between homelessness and prostitution:

> Because I was sexually abused and what have you ... If I knew that it was going to be as bad as it is, the situation I'm in now ... It might sound

sick, but I think I would have rather stayed to get abused at home by my stepfather, and he used to beat me up. I mean I think I would have rather stayed there getting battered and suffering that than suffering out here. Because at least when I was getting beat up, at least I knew I had a house over my head, I had clean clothes the next day, I had a bath ready for me. And I knew the next day I'd have a nice meal [whereas] out here I don't even know when the next square meal is coming in ... That's what it all boils down to, money. If you've got no fixed abode you can't get money off the social. The social won't give you nothing, so you've either got to beg, or you've got to sell yourself ... we do it because we've no choice, it's only our means and way of living. It's the only way we can get our next square meal or ... you know. The more we do ... we get caught, we get fined. It makes it worse because we're going to do it even more to pay the fine (Sarah, 24 years, Manchester).

The classic double bind of prostitution whereby fines for soliciting may only be paid by further engagement in illicit activities is parallelled by the double bind of other subsistence activities associated with street homelessness, in particular begging.

The 'street' as a social space is central to our understanding of the construction of deviant sexualities (Valentine, 1996). All women working as prostitutes are constructed as deviant, but the woman working on the street is more visible, more public and therefore more stigmatised and more regulated than her sister indoors. Similarly there are gradations of deviant male sexualities, with the kerb-crawling heterosexual male client likely to escape police attention, unlike the (heterosexual or homosexual) rent-boy working in the Gay village (Collier, 1995; Waldorf and Murphy, 1990; Donovan, 1992). In turn, the female prostitute is much more closely regulated than her male counterpart: in effect, there is a hierarchy of regulation, with the female prostitute at one extreme, and her male client at the other (Brophy and Smart, 1985). Homeless women seeking to work as prostitutes were not only subjected to regular surveillance by the Vice Squad, and to intermittent 'sweeps' or special operations, but were also routinely excluded from particular areas of the city. Entrepreneurs in the Gay village, for example, banned female (but not male) prostitutes from working outside their businesses, thus helping to spatially confine them to the contiguous red-light district.

Homeless men maintained an ambivalent relationship to the Gay village, identifying the potential for both safety and danger within its confines:

I've seen a lot of lads come from going on the street to going over to be rent boys. 'Cause they've got no money, they've got no decent clothes, they've got no food, they've got empty stomachs all the time, they've got no cigarettes. They can't have a good time, they've got no social life, that's the worst part of being homeless, no social life (Terry).

Many street homeless men were careful to distance themselves from this scenario, their carefulness arising from a reluctance to be identified with the

126

doubly deviant activity of male prostitution. Others, however, expressed a willingness to seek the relative protection of this urban village:

> At night I go to the Gay village 'cause there's a different style of people, I mean people are a lot more caring, they're not full of lager and ready for a fight. Just a different sort of relaxed atmosphere. Anywhere else, I mean you get the lager louts who go up to blokes and try to kick your head in. Then you get gangs of women walking round giving you lots of verbal abuse, know what I mean (Ricky, *Big Issue* vendor).

Survival strategies employed by the street homeless led them almost inexorably into conflict with the settled community, in that such strategies often involve a measure of illegality, and always require the presence of marginalised people within prime urban space. Furthermore, subsistence strategies such as begging, prostitution and sleeping rough increase the likelihood of someone being victimised. The street homeless population is therefore both dangerous and endangered. Perceptions of them as victim as opposed to victimiser depend heavily on the political and moral standpoints adopted by the viewer. Typically, the criminal justice system defines beggars, prostitutes and rough sleepers as criminals, while voluntary agencies and political activists emphasise the victimisation of these groups at the hands of both individuals and the social and political system. Beggars, for example, may be portrayed variously as cynical exploiters of public goodwill or else as victims of social and economic exclusion.

Prostitutes, similarly, may be perceived either as immoral and cynical women, or else as victims of both sexual exploitation and a hypocritical criminal justice system that condemns their actions while benefitting financially from their activities. These groups are the subject of a deep moral ambivalence that, combined with contests over the use of public space, brings them to the forefront of public attention. Informal measures of regulation include the 'nimby' response on the part of residential neighbourhoods, and the victimisation that was discussed in chapter five. Official (police) regulation of street people will be considered in the concluding section to this chapter.

Policing the streets

The police have a dual role in relation to the street homeless population: first, to regulate any illegal subsistence strategies and generally to maintain good order on the streets, and second to protect street people from harassment and criminal victimisation. With regard to policing as regulation, attention is more likely to be directed towards street people when, in pursuit of their daily routines of subsistence they become too visible or too disorderly within prime space, fail to confine themselves to interstitial locales within prime space, or else fail to use such space at marginal times of the day. Arguably, it is the actual or perceived disruptiveness of such routines to mainstream communities that is the key factor in triggering a police response, rather than the legality or illegality of such activities.

Begging and prostitution are both subsistence activities that are regularly practiced within most urban spaces, but it is only periodically that police operations become focused on regulating them. Operation Clean Sweep was undertaken in Manchester in early 1991, with the aim of reducing crimes associated with the activities of rent-boys working the 'meat-rack', and was targeted in particular at theft, drug-related and sexual offences. Police officers reported that rent-boys generally went relatively unregulated, in comparison with the female sex trade, but that Operation Clean Sweep was instigated because of complaints received from owners of local pubs and clubs who were concerned about the impact of the sex trade on their businesses (Donovan, 1992).

Operation Cinderella took place during the first half of 1993, with the aim of reducing street begging in the centre of Manchester. This operation was widely believed by both agency staff and street homeless people to be linked to the city's Olympic bid, and its consequent felt need to project a 'clean' image to the international community. Whether they were accurate in this belief or not, many street homeless people did report having experienced an increase in police activity at around this time, both in relation to begging and, to a lesser extent, sleeping rough.

Others referred to wider changes in the political and legal climate to explain any changes in police policy or activity:

> I think at the moment [August 1994] with the Criminal Justice bill they wanna get through, they gotta prove that crimes are up like. So they go round and they hassle people, and they nick loads of people. And the more arrests and serious charges the better, they've got more chance of getting it through (Kaz).

Some of those who had been moved on for begging and sleeping rough, believed that the police were both reasonable and justified in their actions:

> The police have noticed me a few times ... they sort of look at me and say 'Come on move along now, and if we see you again we'll arrest you', which is quite fair really. Sometimes they are good. Sometimes they give you one warning and other times they just take you away straight away without a warning. I've been lucky to be warned before being arrested (Ricky).

With regard to the second function, policing as protection, experiences and attitudes were similarly of an ambivalent nature. Some actively sought the protection of the police, preferring to accept any attendant risks of regulation in preference to the dangers presented to them by the public. Kaz who, as we have seen, ascribed a political motivation to the number of arrests being made for begging, also appreciated the protective role sometimes adopted by the police:

> I sleep down on the canal basin, at the bottom of Deansgate ... It's quiet, but there's loads of police around there as well ... You're pretty safe

there, except for when they're waking you up to make sure you're not dead (laughs).

In general, however, homeless people noted that they were unlikely to report crimes of violence or sexual assault committed against them to the police. As was documented in chapter five, this decision was made either because they felt that they were likely to be disbelieved, that no further action would be taken, or else that they themselves would come under unwelcome police scrutiny.

Venues on the homelessness circuit are often liable to be omitted from the protective and regulatory gaze of the local police force, being left simply to 'look after their own'. This was the case with the day-centre that was located on the border between Cardboard city and the red-light district:

> The police are fairly good at staying away from the day-centre, in fact sometimes they're too good at staying away! It's been operating for about twenty years and they don't want to know what's going on. If there are any fights they leave it to us to deal with. It's as if they think that it's our fault for opening the centre, so therefore we should deal with any trouble that arises (Jim, day-centre co-ordinator).

Such benign neglect is illustrative of the ambiguous relationship that the police have in relation to the street homeless population: having a responsibility to protect Cardboard citizens, they are also official regulators of the contested space that they inhabit. In turn, street people perceive the police, either alternately or simultaneously, as repressive agents of control or as safeguarders of the dangerous streets.

Conclusion

The stories of Terry, Ricky and Jimmy are illustrative of the efforts of street homeless people to make a space for themselves within an increasingly restrictive political, legal and moral climate. Pete ('people just don't want you on the streets') and Kaz ('they're trying to recreate the city centre') reveal the awareness street people may have of their perceived dangerousness. Homeless women such as Sarah, living and working on the hostile streets, offer the defence against moral attack that 'we do it because we've no choice'. Considerable tension exists for all street people between the awareness of danger and the urgency of their subsistence needs. Survival on the streets requires the successful negotiation of the transgressiveness of being 'matter out of place'. This is achieved primarily by the avoidance of prime space, particularly at prime times of the day. In this way, the liminal street homeless population may subsist by finding places to live and work on the social and spatial margins of urban culture. Rural homeless people such as Dill may have attempted to escape the urban nightmare ('you haven't got any badheads [in Bangor] ... not like in Piccadilly'), only to find that there were few safe spaces for them in rural towns and villages, where their conspicuousness rendered them vulnerable to police attention and to potential victimisation.

A major aim in this chapter has been to analyse the complex relations between the marginal street homeless and the dominant settled populations, an analysis which has been informed by theoretical debates concerning home and homelessness in urban and rural spaces. In particular, there has been an exploration of continually shifting social and physical boundaries, and of geographies of exclusion. An ethnography of rural and urban homelessness has provided local accounts of some of the consequences of these wider processes. Thus, we have seen how the purification of spaces such as the panopticon mall have compounded the already considerable social and physical exclusion of marginal street people. The myth of the rural idyll has been contrasted sharply with the fact of rural homelessness.

The identification of urban fears and unease with the street homeless population has coincided with measures designed to control their presence, such as periodic police 'sweeps' designed to clear the streets of beggars. In contrast to these widespread fears of chaos and disorder, the closely regulated nature of life on the streets has been documented. Moving within their primary domain of Cardboard city, street homeless people in Manchester entered into prime space as infrequently and as inconspicuously as possible, confining themselves to the margins of the cityscape. By such means of self regulation they could hope largely to avoid conflict with the settled community. Contrasting with static conceptualisations of street people (Gans, 1962; Cohen, 1980), a more dynamic picture has been presented of a culture wherein there is active engagement with survivalist spatial practices such as begging, living rough and shadow working. For those homeless within rural space, their survival strategies depended both on careful identity work and on the utilisation of mental maps in order to negotiate local spaces and places. For both the urban and the rural homeless, their use of space is highly contested and subject to continual negotiation and renegotiation.

Epilogue

> It [begging] is not acceptable to be out on the street. There is no justification for it these days. It is a very offensive problem to many people ... We think aggressive begging is a menace. Action has been taken against aggressive begging for some time and will continue (John Major, *Guardian*, 28/5/94).

> I think the basic principle here is to say yes it is right to be intolerant of people homeless on the streets. It's important not to just take [beggars] from one area and dump them in another, but to make sure the facilities are there so that people can be dealt with properly (Tony Blair, *Guardian*, 6/1/97).

Described as having executed a 'hypocritical U-turn' by Conservative Government ministers, Labour leader Tony Blair was at pains to distance himself from Prime Minister Major's stance on 'aggressive begging'. Blair's 'tough on crime, tough on the causes of crime' position was intended to encompass both a commitment to zero tolerance policing strategies and a caring, nineties-style approach to the homeless (*Guardian*, 8/1/97). This debate took place in the run-up to the 1997 general election, and it is still a moot point whether, once in power, Labour policies towards the street homeless have constituted a radical departure - or a continuation - of those of the previous Tory administration.

In any discussion of homelessness it is tempting to say pessimistically that the more things change the more they remain the same. Chapters two and three noted some of the ways in which the homeless have been both romanticised and criminalised over successive centuries, with similar themes, policies and practices emerging over and again. Furthermore, political debate, legislative change and media hype notwithstanding, the exigencies of survival remain much the same as they have always been: the acquisition by some means or other of the essentials of food, clothing and shelter.

Into the late nineties, there has been a continuation of high levels of homelessness, with an estimated quarter of a million people aged 17-25 living in squats and bed and breakfast accommodation alone, not counting hostel-dwellers and rough sleepers. There also has been a consolidation of the 'new homeless' within these numbers, with 41% of the metropolitan young homeless being female, and 32% of them being aged 16-17 years (Centrepoint survey, *Guardian*, 12/1/97).

Key social policy and criminal justice developments of the early-1990s were continued later in the decade. The Rough Sleepers' Initiative was extended from its base in London to other English and some Scottish cities (although not, despite protest, to rural or urban Wales), and zero tolerance police operations spread from the metropolis to cities such as Birmingham and Glasgow. Both initiatives were designed to reduce levels of visible homelessness, and their proponents claim some success in having done so. So there are now apparently fewer people sleeping on the city streets. Yet it seems that many have not gone into hostels as intended (whether or not sufficient spaces ever existed is another question), but have taken to sleeping in disused warehouses and factories in post-industrial cities ('Redundant mills in central Manchester house squatters', *Guardian*, 24/12/97).

The timing of this newspaper article serves to remind us of one perennial feature of homelessness: the seasonal appearance (and subsequent disappearance) each Christmas time of the homeless-person-as-social-victim. Once the crisis cold-weather shelters have closed some return to the streets, while others 'choose' locations such as disused warehouses, motivated by a fear of the violence and harassment they believe they are likely to encounter in hostels. While the extent of these crimes remains unknown (see chapter five), the fact of such victimisation among the homeless is slowly beginning to be acknowledged by politicians: 'the victims of crime are often the poorest and most vulnerable part of the community; indeed, often they are the homeless themselves' (Tony Blair, *Guardian*, 8/1/97).

The public face of our cities continues to change, sometimes slowly and gradually, at other times in more sudden and dramatic ways. A major IRA bomb in June 1996 destroyed or damaged around 1,200 buildings within a quarter of a square mile section of the city of Manchester, including at least half of the Arndale shopping centre. The city recovered and the major shops and other city landmarks have been rebuilt and restored, yet street homeless people remain excluded from the panopticon mall.

Away from the cities, rural discontent and protest commanded media attention following the Countryside marches of 1997 and 1998, and the existence of rural social problems began to be more widely acknowledged. Rural homelessness, it was noted in the quality press, was increasing more rapidly than in urban and metropolitan areas (*Guardian*, 21/2/98). Otherwise it was business as usual: several years after the height of the moral panic concerning new age travellers, they were still routinely being turned away by police in rural areas of Wales, Scotland and England ('Travellers go', *North Wales Weekly News*, 8/5/97).

Amid these social and political developments, young homeless people continue to lead their lives, some caught up in the daily round of subsistence and others looking ahead - with hope and apprehension - to the future. So the final words go to those who told their stories in the prologue: in this reprise they reflect on their present and future lives.

Dill - the rural idyll?

I don't like the cities 'cause I get a load of shit, 'specially being on the streets. It's quieter here, you've got homeless people in the town, but you haven't got any badheads. Not like in Piccadilly ... I was getting loads of hassle when I was in Manchester and so I thought 'Bangor, a small town, somewhere quiet by the sea'. It's all right here, I try to keep myself to myself 'cause that's what I'm used to. I like to work an area out, and when I have worked it out I like to move again, else I get bored with it ... It's better here than the cities, 'cause like Piccadilly can be tough.

Ellie - the travelling life

I'm staying with a friend in Anglesey at the moment, although I'm going travelling pretty soon. Then I'll come back here, because as I said I like to make Bangor my base. Most of the time I'm travelling. I come back here and I spend maybe a few weeks here, and go back out again. Basically I make myself a destination, and then I just go in that direction, and stop in towns. Sometimes I stop in a town for a week, depends if I make any friends or not. I just hitch on my own, with my dog for company. He's the best.

Katy - institutionalisation

They get you a flat at the end of twelve months. But I don't really want a flat, I want shared or sheltered [accommodation], 'cause I'm used to being like around a lot of people, so I'd prefer that. I wouldn't like my own flat, 'cause even though I've got the baby I'd still be scared to be on my own ... The hostel is an institution, and all the hostels I've been in are institutions, and that's why I don't want my own flat, because I've been institutionalised for so long, three years, and always depended on people really. I feel safe in a hostel, but there again even though there's people around, you still feel alone. I don't really think you can predict the future, but I would like a nice steady job, my own flat, and not being scared to stay at home, and being a career woman I think, that's what I would want.

Kaz - groundhog day

How do I spend my days? I'll sell the [Big] Issue and then I'd have a drink ... then I'd ... (long pause) ... phew ... nothing, don't know like, find a few mates and sit around. Sometimes if there's no one around, go in library and get something, library's all right. Just sit round like, depends if it's sunny. When it's cold it's just go in a cafe and spend as much as you can on cups of tea and make them last you.

Michael - dealing with racism

No I never think about the future me, it doesn't bother me. In five year's time I'll still be doing what I'm doing now. Depends on how the situation changes 'cause I'll never get the money to leave the country. I'll never have the money to do that. Unless we get a fascist party in government here, we'll be repatriated anyway, that's what I think. Whether we like it or not. They'll give us a couple of thousand pound and send us all off to Africa. They can give me a couple of thousand pound and I'll go to Africa but I won't stay there, I'll bugger off to somewhere else. South-east Asia, where the money's worth a lot more. Maybe in a year's time I might meet a girl and I'll settle down, you never know. Or I could be doing the same but I'll never end up a drunken alcoholic on the streets, I mean that's one thing I don't want to do.

Shanaz - victim and survivor

I've been here [in the hostel] for four weeks. And now I'm just really trying to get myself into college, get meself a career, going to learn to drive. Being here I can be myself now. There's only the pain of me kids, but apart from that I'm happy with life now. I am eventually happy with life. Everyone thinks you're happy because of his acting, and me not saying nothing to nobody. But who knows what's going on inside the house? Only me.

Glossary

Abraham (abram) man	a beggar falsely claiming to have been an inmate of the Bedlam asylum (Tudor and Stuart times); a veteran tramp (inter-war years)
Autem mort	a beggar woman, according to Harman married but not faithful to one partner
Bawdy-basket	a woman who begs and steals clothes from hedges; like the *autem mort* Harman describes the *bawdy-basket* as 'lewd and lecherous'
Cant	(n) beggar's language (16th C); jargon of criminals and vagabonds (17-18th C); (v) to beg
Charity irritator	one who makes false claims for support to charities
Chats	the gallows
Clying the jerk	to be whipped
Cock Lorell	traditional name given to a leader of vagrants
Counterfeit crank	one who begs for alms by pretending to be epileptic
Dell	a young beggar woman, 'able for generation and not yet broken' (Harman)
Demander for glimmer	mostly women, someone who asks for a light and then demands money for the goods thus claimed to have been burned and spoiled
Doxy	a sexually experienced but unmarried woman who

	allies herself with *upright men*, and/or who works as a prostitute
Draw-latch	a burglar
Dummerer	one who claims to be unable to speak, in order to request alms; Harman alleged that they were mostly Welsh people who falsely claimed to be unable to speak English
Faitor	a fortune-teller; a gypsy
Flatty	one who does not understand beggar's cant or tramp jargon
Frater	a mendicant friar, possibly carrying a false licence to beg
Gwragedd cawsa	female beggars in medieval North Wales
Harman-beck	a parish constable
Harmans	the stocks
Haystack queen	an impoverished prostitute
High flyer	a sophisticated beggar
Hooker	someone who stole clothes from houses by means of a hooked staff
Irish toil	a supposed pedlar who takes money without delivering the goods
Jacks men	tramps who drink methylated spirits
Jarkmen	a forger of licences and passports, for which a knowledge of Latin was required
Kinchin co	a young male beggar
Kinchin mort	a young woman, before she is given to an *upright man* to be 'broken' and thus to become a *dell*
Kit Callot	traditional name given to (English, male) rogues
Land squatter	beggar with a particular pitch or territory
Milestone inspector	euphemism for tramp

Moon-men	gypsies; lunatics (real or faked)
Mugger	itinerant pedlar
Palliard	also known as *clapperdudgeons*, the *palliard* begged for food which he later sold for profit; he worked together with his *doxy* and Harman says that the majority of *palliards* were Welshmen
Patrico	an itinerant priest
Pedlars' French	the language of rogues and vagabonds
Prater	a tramp parson, collecting donations for pseudo-religious work
Prigger of prancers	a horse-thief
Queer-ken	a prison-house
Robardsman	a thief in the tradition of Robin Hood
Rogue	not so 'stout or hardy' as the *upright man*, the *rogue* feigns ill-health in order to beg
Ruffler	one who pretends to have been a soldier in order to beg; someone who steals from 'wayfaring men and market women'
Scranbag	one who begs for their daily bread; someone low down in the hierarchy of beggars
Slummer	philanthropists or evangelists who made a practice of visiting lodging houses
Son of rest	humorous self-description among tramps
Stalling to the rogue	performing an initiation ceremony among beggars
Sturdy beggar	one of the earliest categories of rogues and vagabonds, predating Harman
Tom O'Bedlam	fictional characterisation of the *abraham man*
Upright man	a leader among rogues and vagabonds; one who is responsible for *stalling to the rogue*, initiating others into a life of begging

Vagabond	one of the earliest categories of rogues, predating Harman
Walking mort	unmarried beggar woman, falsely claiming to be a widow
Wild rogue	a born rogue or vagabond

Sources: *Harman (1566); Dekker (1612); Burn (1855); Rose (1988)*

Bibliography

Abu-Lughod, J.L. (1994), *From Urban Village to East Village*, Oxford: Blackwell.

Alder, C. (1991), 'Victims of violence: the case of homeless youth', *Australia and New Zealand Journal of Criminology*, 24:1-14, March.

Allsop, K. (1967), *Hard Travellin': The Hobo and His History*, New York: New American Library.

Altman, I. (1975), *The Environment and Social Behaviour*, Monterey, California: Brooks/Cole.

Altman, I. and Werner, C. M. (1985), *Home Environments*, New York: Plenum Press.

Anderson, N. (1923), *The Hobo: the Sociology of the Homeless Man*, Chicago: University of Chicago Press.

Anon, (1703), *Hell Upon Earth*, London: pamphlet.

Anon, (1725), *A New Canting dictionary*, London: pamphlet.

Anon, (1754), *The Scoundrel's Dictionary*, London: J Brownell.

Anon, (nd.), *The Canting Academy*, London: Matthew Drew.

Archard, P. (1979), *Vagrancy, Alcoholism and Social Control*, London: Macmillan.

Auden, W. H. (1966), *About the House*, London: Faber and Faber.

Awdeley, J. (1561), *The Fraternity of Vagabonds*, London: pamphlet.

Aydelotte, F. (1913), *Elizabethan Rogues and Vagabonds*, Oxford: Clarendon Press.

Aye Maung, N. (1995), *Young People, Victimisation and the Police: BCS Findings on Experiences and Attitudes of 12 to 15 year olds*, Home Office Research Study 140, London: HMSO.

Bahr, H. M. (1973), *Skid Row: an Introduction to Disaffiliation*, New York: Oxford University Press.

Bammer, A. (1992), Editorial 'The question of home', *New Formations*, Summer, 17:vii-xi.

Bammer, A. (ed.) (1994), *Displacements: Cultural Identities in Question*, Bloomington and Indianapolis: Indiana University Press.

Baumann, D.J., Beauvais, C., Grigsby, C. and Schultz, F.D. (1985), *The Austin Homeless: Final Report Provided to the Hogg Foundation for Mental Health*, Austin: Hogg Foundation for Mental Health.

Beier, A. L. (1985), *Masterless Men: The Vagrancy Problem in England 1560-1640*, London: Methuen.

Bell, I. A. (1991), *Literature and Crime in Augustan England*, London: Routledge.

Beresford, P. (1979), 'The public presentation of vagrancy', in T.Cook (ed.), *Vagrancy: Some New Perspectives*, London: Academic Press.

Bittner, E. (1967), 'The police on Skid Row: a study of peace keeping', *American Sociological Review*, 32:699-715.

Brophy, J. and Smart, C. (eds.) (1985), *Women in Law*, London: Routledge.

Bruns, R. A. (1980), *Knights of the Road: a Hobo History*, New York: Methuen.

Bunce, M. (1994), *The Countryside Idyll: Anglo-American Images of Landscape*, London: Routledge.

Bunston, T. and Breton, M. (1990), 'The eating patterns and problems of homeless women', *Women and Health*, 16(1):43-62.

Burn, J.D. (1855), *The Autobiography of a Beggar Boy*, London: William Tweedie.

Carlen, P. (1988), *Women, Crime and Poverty*, Buckingham: Open University Press.

Carlen, P. (1996), *Jigsaw: a Political Criminology of Youth Homelessness*, Buckingham: Open University Press.

Carlen, P. and Wardhaugh, J. (1992), *Shropshire Single Homelessness Survey*, Shrewsbury: Shropshire Probation/Keele University.

Chambliss, W. (1964), 'A sociological analysis of the law of vagrancy', *Social Problems*, 12:67-77.

Chambliss, W. (1976), 'The state and criminal law', in W. Chambliss and M. Mankoff (eds.), *Whose Law? What Order? A Conflict Approach to Criminology*, New York: John Wiley.

Chandler, F. W. (1907), *The Literature of Roguery*, New York: Macmillan.

Chesterton, A. (1926), *In Darkest London*, New York: Macmillan.

Chesterton, A. (1928), *Women of the Underworld*, London: Stanley Paul & Co.

Ching, B. and Creed G. W. (eds.) (1997), *Knowing Your Place: Rural Identity and Cultural Hierarchy*, Routledge: New York.

Cloke, P. and Little, J. (1997), 'Introduction: other countrysides' in P.Cloke and J.Little (eds.), *Contested Countryside Cultures*, London: Routledge.

Cloke, P., Goodwin, M. and Milbourne, P. (1997), *Rural Wales: Community and Marginalization*, Cardiff: University of Wales Press.

Cohen, B. (1980), *Deviant Street Networks: Prostitution in New York City*, Massachusetts: Lexington Books.

Cohen, S. (ed.) (1971), *Images of Deviance*, London: Penguin.

Cohen, S. and Taylor, L. (1972), *Psychological Survival*, Harmondsworth: Penguin.

Cohen, S. and Taylor, L. (1992), *Escape Attempts: the Theory and Practice of Resistance to Everyday Life*, London: Routledge.

Collier, R. (1995), *Masculinity, Law and the Family*, London: Routledge.

Collins, P. (1962), *Dickens and Crime*, London: Macmillan.

Cooper, C. (1974), 'The house as a symbol of self', in J. Lang, C. Burnett, W. Moleski and D. Vachon (eds.), *Designing for Human Behavior*, Stroudsberg, Penn.: Dowden, Hutchinson and Ross.

Corrigan, P., Jones, T., and Young, J. (1989), 'Rights and obligations', *New Socialist*, Feb-March, pp. 16-17.

Cretney, A. and Davis, G. (1995), *Punishing Violence*, London: Routledge.

Crouse, J.M. (1986), *The Homeless Transient in the Great Depression: New York State 1929-1941*, New York: State University of New York Press.

Daly, G. (1996), *Homeless: Policies, Strategies and Lives on the Streets*, London: Routledge.

Darke, J. (1994), 'Women and the meaning of home', in R. Gilroy and R. Woods (eds.), *Housing Women*, London: Routledge.

Davies, T. (1980s), 'The Anglesey hunt: 1895-1934', *Oral History*, Anglesey: Llangefni archives, document: WM/T.69/2.

Davis, J., Grant, R. and Locke, A. (1994), *Out of Site, Out of Mind: New Age Travellers and the Criminal Justice and Public Order Bill*, London: Children's Society.

Davis, M. (1990), *City of Quartz: Excavating the Future in Los Angeles*, New York: Verso.

Deakin, M. and Willis, J. (1976), *Johnny Go Home*, London: Futura.

Dekker, T. (1608), *Lantern and Candlelight*, London: John Busbie.

Dekker, T. (1612), *O Per Se O*, London: John Busbie.

Denning, M. (1986), 'Beggars and thieves: *The Beggar's Opera* as crime drama', in P.Humm, P. Stignant and P. Widdowson (eds.), *Popular Fictions: Essays in Literature and History*, London: Methuen.

Dibblin, J. (1991), *Wherever I Lay My Hat: Young Women and Homelessness*, London: Shelter.

Dickens, C. (1853), 'Home for homeless women' in *Household Words, 23 April. Miscellaneous Papers 369*, London: Biographical Edition.

Donovan, K. (1992), *Hidden From View*, Birmingham: West Midlands Police.

Douglas, A. and Gilroy, R. (1994), 'Young women and homelessness', in R. Gilroy and R. Woods (eds.), *Housing Women*, London: Routledge.

Douglas, M. (1964; 1992), *Purity and Danger: An Analysis of Concepts of Pollution and Taboo*, London: Routledge.

Douglas, T. (1995), *Scapegoats: Transferring Blame*, London: Routledge.

Dovey, K. (1985), 'Home and homelessness', in I. Altman and C. Werner, *Home Environments*, New York: Plenum Press.

Duncan, J. S. (1983), 'Men without property: the tramp's classification and use of urban space', in R. W. Lake, *Readings in Urban Analysis: Perspective on Urban Form and Structure*, Centre for Urban Policy Research: USA.

Ellis, S. C. (1987), 'Observations of Anglesey life through the Quarter Sessions Rolls 1860-1869', *Anglesey Antiquarian Society Transactions 1986-7*, Anglesey: Llangefni archives.

Erlam, A. and Brown, M. (1976), *Catering For Homeless Workers*, London: CHAR and Low Pay Unit.

Fielding, H. (1743), *The Life of Jonathan Wild*, Oxford: Oxford University Press.

Fleisher, M. (1995), *Beggars and Thieves: Lives of Urban Street Criminals*, Madison: University of Wisconsin Press.

Foucault, M. (1980), *The History of Sexuality*, New York: Vintage Books.

Gans, H. J. (1962), *The Urban Villagers: Group and Class in the Life of Italian-Americans*, New York: Free Press.

Garrett, G. R. and Bahr, H.M. (1976), 'The family backgrounds of Skid Row women', *Signs: Journal of Women and Culture*, 2(2):369-81.

Gay, J. (1728; 1969), *The Beggar's Opera*, London: Edward Arnold.

Genn, H. (1988), 'Multiple victimisation', in M. Maguire and J. Pointing, *Victims of Crime: A New Deal?*, Buckingham: Open University Press.

Giddens, A. (1990), *The Consequences of Modernity*, Cambridge: Polity.

Gilbert, N. (ed.) (1993), *Researching Social Life*, London: Sage.

Glasser, I. (1988), *More Than Bread: Ethnography of a Soup Kitchen*, Tuscaloosa: University of Alabama Press.

Goffman, E. (1959), *The Presentation of Self in Everyday Life*, London: Penguin.

Goffman, E. (1961), *Asylums*, New York: Anchor Books.

Goffman, E. (1971), *Relations in Public: Microstudies of the Public Order*, London: Allen Lane.

Goffman, E. (1972), *Encounters: Two Studies in Social Interaction*, London: Penguin.

Golden, S. (1992), *The Women Outside: Meanings and Myths of Homelessness*, Berkeley: University of California Press.

Gordon, M. (1991), *Good Boys and Dead Girls and Other Essays*, London: Viking.

Gould, J. and White, R. (1974), *Mental Maps*, Harmondsworth: Penguin.

Grant, R. J. K. (1988), *On the Parish: An Illustrated Source Book on the Care of the Poor under the Old Poor Law*, Glamorgan: Glamorgan archive service.

Greene, R. (1591), *A Notable Discovery of Cozenage*, London: Thomas Nelson.

Greenwood, J. (1866), 'A night in the workhouse', *Pall Mall Gazette*.

Gregor, T. (1977), *Mehinaku: The Drama of Daily Life in a Brazilian Indian Village*, Chicago, Illinois:University of Chicago Press.

Greve, J., Page, D. and Greve, S. (1971), *Homelessness in London*, London: HMSO.

Grose, F. (1796; 1992), *Classical Dictionary of the Vulgar Tongue*, New York: Dorset.

Hagan, J. and McCarthy, B. (1997), *Mean Streets: Youth Crime and Homelessness*, Cambridge: Cambridge University Press.

Hagan, J. and McCarthy, B. (n.d.), 'Double jeopardy: the abuse and punishment of homeless youth', Unpublished paper, Universities of Toronto and Victoria.

Hall, S., Jefferson, T., Critcher, C. and Roberts, B. (1978), *Policing the Crisis: Mugging, the State and Law and Order*, London: Macmillan.

Hammersley, M. and Atkinson, P. (1995), *Ethnography: Principles in Practice*, London: Routledge.

Harman, T. (1566), *A Caveat for Common Cursitors Vulgarly Called Vagabonds*, London: William Griffith.

Harper, D. (1979), 'Life on the road', in J.Wagner (ed.), *Images of Information: Still Photography in the Social Sciences*, London: Sage.

Harper, D. (1982), *Good Company*, Chicago: Chicago University Press.

Harvey, D. (1989), *The Condition of Postmodernity*, Oxford: Blackwell.

Hawes, D. and Perez, B. (1995), *The Gypsy and the State: the Ethnic Cleansing of British Society*, Bristol University: School for Advanced Urban Studies.

Heidegger, M. (1962), *Being and Time*, New York: Harper and Row.

Hendessi, M. (1992), *4 in 10: Report on Young Women Who Become Homeless as a Result of Sexual Abuse*, London: CHAR

Higgs, M. (1905), *Three Nights in Women's Lodging Houses*, Oldham: pamphlet (private circulation).

Higgs, M. (1906), *Glimpses into the Abyss*, London: P.S.King & Son.

Higgs, M. (1914), *My Brother the Tramp*, London: Student Christian Movement.

Hindelang, M.J., Gottfredson, M.R. and Garofalo, J. (1978), *Victims of Personal Crime: an Empirical Foundation for a Theory of Personal Victimisation*, Cambridge, Massachusetts: Ballinger.

Hoch, C. and Slayton, R.A. (1992), *New Homeless and Old: Community and the Skid Row Hotel*, Philadelphia: Temple University Press.

Hoigard, C. and Finstad, L. (1992), *Backstreets: Prostitution, Money and Love*, Oxford: Polity Press.

hooks, b. (1991), *Yearning: Race, Gender, and Cultural Politics*, London: Turnaround.

Hope, M. and Young, J. (1986), *The Faces of Homelessness*, Toronto: Lexington.

Hotten, J. C. (1922), *The Slang Dictionary*, London: Chatto & Windus.

Hotten, J. C. and Thomas, D. B. (eds.) (1932), *The Book of Vagabonds and Beggars*, London: John Camden Hotten (originally published in 1492 by Martin Luther as *Liber Vagatorum*).

Hough, M. (1990), 'Threats: findings from the British Crime Survey', *International Review of Victimology*, 1:169-180.

Hunter, A. (1985), 'Private, parochial and public social orders: the problem of crime and incivility in urban communities', in G. D. Suttles and M. N. Zald (eds.), *The Challenge of Social Control: Citizenship and Institution Building in Modern Society - Essays in Honor of Morris Janowitz*, Norwood, N.J.: Ablex Publishing Company.

Hutson, S. and Liddiard, M. (1994), *Youth Homelessness: the Construction of a Social Issue*, London: Macmillan.

Illich, I. (1981), *Shadow Work*, Boston: Marion Boyars.

Johnson, E. (ed.) (1953), *Letters from Charles Dickens to Angela Burdett-Coutts*, London.

Jones, D. J. V. (1977), 'A dead loss to the community: the criminal vagrant in mid-nineteenth-century Wales', *The Welsh History Review*, 8:312-344.

Jones, D. J. V. (1992), *Crime in Nineteenth Century Wales*, Cardiff: University of Wales Press.

Judges, A.V. (ed.) (1930), *The Elizabethan Underworld*, London: George Routledge and Sons.

Jung, C. G. (1967), *Memories, Dreams and Reflections*, London: Fontana.

Junker, B. (1960), *Field Work*, Chicago, Illinois: University of Chicago Press.

Kaler, A. K. (1991), *The Picara: from Hera to Fantasy Heroine*, Ohio: Bowling Green State University Popular Press.

Katz, J. (1988), *Seductions of Crime: Moral and Sensual Attractions in Doing Evil*, New York: Basic Books.

Keane, J. (1996), *Reflections on Violence*, London: Verso.

Keating, P. (ed.) (1976), *Into Unknown England, 1866-1913: Selections from the Social Explorers*, London: Fontana/Collins.

Kelling, G. L. (1995), *Fixing 'Broken Windows': Order and Individualism in American Cities*, New York: Praeger.

Kelly, J.T. (1985), 'Trauma: with the example of the San Francisco shelter programs', in P.W. Brickner et al (eds.), *Health Care of Homeless People*, New York: Springer.

Kelly, M. (1990), 'Using the law to punish the homeless and hungry', *Childright*, 68:6-7, July/August.

Kennedy, W. (1983), *Ironweed*, New York: Viking Press.

Kinney, A.F. (1990), *Rogues, Vagabonds and Sturdy Beggars: A New Gallery of Tudor and Early Stuart Literature*, Amherst: University of Massachusetts Press.

Kirkwood, C. (1993), *Leaving Abusive Partners*, London: Sage.

Kitch, C. (1996), *Pavement for my Pillow*, London: Orion.

Korosec-Serfaty, P. (1985), 'Experience and use of the dwelling', in I. Altman and C. Werner, *Home Environments*, New York: Plenum Press.

Kozol, J. (1988), *Rachel And Her Children: Homeless Families In America*, New York: Fawcett Columbine.

Kufeldt, K. and Nimmo, M. (1987), 'Youth on the street: abuse and neglect in the eighties', *Child Abuse and Neglect*, 11:531-43.

Landau, S.F. and Freeman-Lang, K.E. (1990), 'Classifying victims: a proposed multidimensional victimological typology', *International Review of Victimology*, 1(3):267-86.

Laslett, P. (1965), *The World We Have Lost: Life in Preindustrial England*, New York: Scribner's.

Lawrence, M. (1995), 'Rural homelessness: a geography without a geography', *Journal of Rural Studies*, 11(3):293-307.

Lee, B.A. (1989), 'Homelessness in Tennessee', in J.A. Momeni (ed.), *Homelessness in the United States: State Surveys*, Westport, Connecticut: Greenwood Press.

Lifton, R.J. (1992), 'Victims and survivors', in B. Giamo and J. Grunberg (eds.), *Beyond Homelesness: Frames of Reference*, Iowa City, IA: University of Iowa Press.

Lofland, L. (1973), *A World of Strangers: Order and Action in Urban Public Space*, New York: Free Press.

Loughrey, B. and Treadwell, T. O. (1986), *John Gay: The Beggar's Opera*, London: Penguin.

MacGill, P. (1914; 1985), *Children of The Dead End: Autobiography of a Navvy*, London: Caliban.

Maguire, M. and Pointing, J. (eds.) (1988), *Victims of Crime: a New Deal?*, Buckingham: Open University Press.

Malson, H. (1997), 'Anorexic bodies and the discursive production of feminine excess', in J. M. Ussher (ed.), *Body Talk: the Material and Discursive Regulation of Sexuality, Madness and Reproduction*, London: Routledge.

Martin, E. (1987), *The Woman in the Body*, Boston: Beacon Press.

Mason, J. (1996), *Qualitative Researching*, London: Sage.

Massey, D. (1991), 'A global sense of place', *Marxism Today*, pp. 24-9, June.

Massey, D. (1992), 'A place called home?', in *The Question of 'Home'*, *New Formations*, 17:3-15, Summer.

Massey, D. (1994), *Space, Place and Gender*, Cambridge: Polity Press.

Mawby, R. I. and Walklate, S. (1994), *Critical Victimology*, London: Sage.

McSheehy, W. (1979), *Skid Row*, Boston: G.K.Hall.

Merton, R. K (1968), *Social Theory and Social Structure*, New York: Free Press.

Milbourne, P. (ed.) (1997), *Revealing Rural Others: Representation, Power and Identity in the Countryside*, London: Pinter.

Mingay, G. E. (1989), *The Rural Idyll*, London: Routledge.

Murdoch, A. (1994), *We Are Human Too: A Study of People Who Beg*, London: Crisis.

Murray, H. (1986), 'Time in the Streets', in J.Ericcksson and C.Wilhelm (eds.), *Housing the Homeless*, Rutgers, N.J.: Center for Urban Policy.

Newton, C. (1994), 'Gender theory and prison sociology: using theories of masculinity to interpret the sociology of prisons for men', *Howard Journal of Criminal Justice*, 33(3):193-202.

North Wales Police, (1998), 'A brief history of the force', World wide web (http://dspace.dial.pipex.com/nwp/ehist.html), pp. 1-4, 13 January.

O'Connell Davidson, J. and Layder, D. (1994), *Methods, Sex and Madness*, London: Routledge.

O'Connor, P. (1963), *Vagrancy: Ethos and Actuality*, Harmondsworth: Penguin.

Okely, J. (1983), *The Traveller-Gypsies*, Cambridge: Cambridge University Press.

Orwell, G. (1933), *Down and Out in Paris and London*, New York: Harcourt, Brace, Jovanovich.

Park, R. E. (1926), 'The urban community as a spatial and a moral order', in E. W. Burgess (ed.), *The Urban Community*, Chicago: University of Chicago Press.

Parton, N. (1985), *The Politics of Child Abuse*, London: Macmillan.

Partridge, E. (1950; 1995), *Dictionary of the Underworld*, London: Wordsworth Editions.

Passaro, J. (1996), *The Unequal Homeless: Men on the Streets, Women in their Place*, London: Routledge.

Philo, C. (1992), 'Neglected rural geographies: a review', *Journal of Rural Studies*, 8(2):193-207.

Pitch, T. (1995), *Limited Responsibilities: Social Movements and Criminal Justice*, London: Routledge.

Pocock, D. C. D. and Hudson, R. (1978), *Images of the Urban Environment*, London: Macmillan.

Pound, J. (1971), *Poverty and Vagrancy in Tudor England*, London: Longman Group Limited.

Powers, J., Eckenrode, J. and Jaklitsch, B. (1990), 'Maltreatment among runaway and homeless youth', *Child Abuse and Neglect*, 14: 87-98.

Randall, G. and Brown, S. (1993), *The Rough Sleepers' Initiative: an Evaluation*, London: HMSO.

Rendell, R. (1996), *Keys to the Street*, London: Random House.

Rex, J. and Moore, R. (1967), *Race, Community and Conflict*, Oxford: Oxford University Press.

Rid, S. (1612), *Art of Juggling*, London: pamphlet.

Robson, P. and Poustie, M. (1996), *Homeless People and the Law*, Edinburgh: Butterworths.

Rock, P. (1974), 'Foreword', in I. Paulus, *The Search for Pure Food: A Sociology of Legislation in Britain*, London: Robertson.

Rose, E. (1965; 1997), 'The unattached society: an account of the life on Larimer Street among homeless men', *Ethnographic Studies*, 1:1-93.

Rose, L. (1988), *Rogues and Vagabonds: Vagrant Underworld in Britain 1815-1985*, London: Routledge.

Rossi, P., Wright, J.D., Fischer, G.A. and Willis, G. (1987), 'The urban homeless: estimating composition and size', *Science*, 235:1336-41.

Roth, D., Bean, G.J., Lust, N. and Traian, S. (1985), *Homelessness in Ohio: A Study of People In Need*, Ohio: Ohio Department of Mental Health.

Rowe, S. and Wolch, J. (1990), 'Social networks in time and space: homeless women in Skid Row, Los Angeles', *Annals of the Association of American Geographers*, 80(2):184-204.

Russell, B. G. (1991), *Silent Sisters: A Study of Homeless Women*, New York: Taylor and Francis.

Sandford, J. (1971), *Down and Out in Britain*, London: Peter Owen.

Sandford, J. (1976), *Edna the Inebriate Woman*, London: Marion Boyars.

Sargado, G. (1977), *The Elizabethan Underworld*, London: J. M. Dent & Sons.

Saunders, P. (1981), *Social Theory and the Urban Question*, London: Hutchinson.

Saxby, M. (c.1801), *Memoirs of Mary Saxby*, London: pamphlet.

Sennett, R. (1996), *The Uses of Disorder: Personal Identity and City Life*, London: Faber and Faber.

Shakespeare, W. (1606; 1961), *The Tragedy of King Lear*, London: Penguin.

Shaw, G. B. (1995), 'Women in the home', in J. M. and M. J. Cohen, *Dictionary of Twentieth-Century Quotations*, London: Penguin.

Shelter Cymru, (1998), *Rough Sleepers: A Rural Issue?*, Cardiff: Gwynedd County Council/Shelter Cymru.

Shields, R. (1991), *Places on the Margin: Alternative Geographies of Modernity*, London: Routledge.

Short, B. (ed.) (1992), *The English Rural Community: Image and Analysis*, Cambridge: Cambridge University Press.

Sibley, D. (1995), *Geographies of Exclusion: Society and Difference in the West*, London: Routledge.

Sim, J. (1994), 'Tougher than the rest? Men in prison', in T. Newburn and E.A. Stanko (eds.), *Just Boys Doing Business? Men, Masculinities and Crime*, London: Routledge.

Smailes, J. (1994), 'The struggle has never been simply about bricks and mortar: lesbians'experience of housing' in R. Gilroy and R. Woods (eds.), *Housing Women*, London: Routledge.

Snow, D. A. and Anderson, L. (1993), *Down on Their Luck: A Study of Homeless Street People*, Berkeley: University of California Press.

Soja, E. (1997), 'Planning in/for Postmodernity', in G. Benko and U. Strohmayer, *Interpreting Modernity and Post Modernity*, Oxford: Blackwell.

Sorokin, P. A. and Zimmerman, C. C. (1929), *Principles of Rural-urban Sociology*, New York: Hinny Holt.

Sparks, R. F., Genn, H. G. and Dodd, D. J. (1977), *Surveying Victims*, London: Wiley.

Spradley, J. P. (1970), *You Owe Yourself a Drunk: An Ethnography of Urban Nomads*, Boston: Little Brown and Company.

Stallard, J. H. (1866), *The Female Vagrant and her Lodging*, London: pamphlet.

Stein, M., Rees, G. and Frost, N. (1994), *Running - The Risk: Young People on the Streets of Britain Today*, Leeds: Children's Society.

Taylor, I., Evans, K. and Fraser, P. (1996), *A Tale Of Two Cities: Global Change, Local Feeling and Everyday Life in the North of England*, London: Routledge.

Thomas, Mrs. (1980s), *Untitled oral history*, Anglesey: Llangefni archives, document: WM/T/89.

Tönnies, F. (1955), *Community and Association*, London: Routledge and Kegan Paul

Turner, V. (1974), *Dramas, Fields and Metaphors*, Ithaca, N.Y.: Cornell University Press.

Turner, V. (1979), *Process, Performance and Pilgrimage*, New Delhi: Concept.

Valentine, G. (1996), '(Re)negotiating the "heterosexual street": lesbian productions of space', in N. Duncan (ed.), *Bodyspace: Destabilizing Geographies of Gender and Sexuality*, London: Routledge.

Van Gennep, A. (1960), *The Rites of Passage*, Chicago: University of Chicago Press.

Vander Kooi, R. C. (1973), 'The Mainstem: Skid Row revisited', *Society*, 10:64-71.

Von Hentig, H. (1948), *The Criminal and his Victim*, New York: Praeger.

Wagner, D. (1993), *Checkerboard Square: Culture and Resistance in a Homeless Community*, Colorado: Westview Press.

Waldorf, D. and Murphy, S. (1990), 'Intravenous drug use and syringe-sharing practices of call men and hustlers', in M. A. Plant (ed.), *Aids, Drugs and Prostitution*, London: Routledge.

Walklate, S. (1995), *Gender and Crime*, London: Prentice Hall/Harvester Wheatsheaf.

Wallace, S. E. (1965), *Skid Row as a Way of Life*, New York: Harper.

Wallich-Clifford, A. (1974), *No Fixed Abode*, London, Macmillan.

Wardhaugh, J. (1996), '"Homeless in Chinatown": deviance and social control in Cardboard city', *Sociology*, 30(4):701-716.

Wardhaugh, J. (1999), 'The unaccommodated woman: home, homelessness and identity', *Sociological Review*, 47(1):91-109.

Watson, R. (1997), 'Prologue to "The Unattached Society: an account of the life on Larimer Street among homeless men"', *Ethnographic Studies*, 1:iv-xii.

Watson, S. with Austerberry, H. (1986), *Housing and Homelessness: A Feminist Perspective*, London: Routledge and Kegan Paul.

Whitbeck, L. and Simons, R. (1990), 'Life on the streets: the victimization of runaway and homeless adolescents', *Youth and Society*, 22: 108-25.

Wilkinson, T. (1981), *Down and Out*, London: Quartet.

Wilson, E. (1991), *The Sphinx in the City: Urban Life, the Control of Disorder and Women*, London: Virago.

Wilson, E. (1995), 'The invisible *flâneur*', in S. Watson and K. Gibson (eds.), *Postmodern Cities and Spaces*, Oxford: Basil Blackwell.

Winstanley, L. (1909), *The Scholar Vagabond*, London: Hutchinson and Co.

Wiseman, J. (1973), *Stations Of The Lost: The Treatment of Skid Row Alcoholics*, Chicago: University of Chicago Press.

Wolff, J. (1993), 'On the road again: metaphors of travel in cultural criticism', *Cultural Studies*, 7:224-39.

Woolf, V. (1929), *A Room of One's Own*, London: Hogarth Press.

Workhouse Committee, (1895), *Untitled document* (dated 29/11/1895), document: WG/3/70, Anglesey: Llangefni Archives.

Young, J. (1988), 'Risk of crime and fear of crime: a realist critique of survey-based assumptions', in M. Maguire and J. Pointing. (eds.) (1988), *Victims of Crime: a New Deal?*, Buckingham: Open University Press.

Index

holy poverty, 34
home, 1, 3, 5-6, 10, 12-14, 17, 20, 46, 62-3, 67, 71, 73, 75-86, 90-1, 93-4, 98-9, 102, 110-11, 113, 119, 123, 126, 130, 133, 139, 141, 145-6, 148
homelessness, 1, 6, 10, 17 -22, 25, 27, 32-3, 35, 40-2, 47, 49, 64, 66, 70, 72-83, 85-7, 89-91, 101-2, 104, 107, 109, 113, 115, 117-18, 120, 122, 125-6, 129-32, 141, 144, 148
homelessness circuit, 10, 18, 25, 27, 113, 115, 117-18, 120, 125, 129
Housing (Homeless Persons) Act (1977), 41
Housing Act (1996), 41

identity work, 83-4, 110, 130
Ireland, 43, 55, 63-4

King Lear, 73, 75, 146
Kitch, Chris, 72, 144

legal discourse, 35-6, 49
Liber Vagatorum, 50, 55, 143
liminality, 74, 104, 117, 123
Liverpool, 10, 38
lodging-houses, 40, 58, 69

MacGill, Patrick, 64-66, 144
Major, John, 25, 37, 101, 131
Manchester, 1-3, 7, 9-10, 12, 18, 23-4, 28-30, 83-4, 92, 94-5, 97, 99, 103-4, 111-14, 118, 122-3, 126, 128, 130, 132-3
marginality, 21, 102, 113, 117-18
meat-rack, 128
mental maps, 45, 110, 125, 130
Morris Report (1975), 40

National Assistance, 40
new age travellers, 18, 36, 55, 104, 132
new homeless, 40-1, 72, 132
New Vagrancy Act, 41

North Wales, 17, 33, 42-44, 46, 61, 105, 107, 121, 132, 136, 145

Operation Cinderella, 128
Operation Clean Sweep, 37, 128
Other, 9, 34, 62, 70, 79, 85, 94, 97, 98, 104, 109, 125, 142

participant observation, 19, 22-3, 26, 60
phenomenology, 76
picaresque literature, 52, 59, 63
Piccadilly Gardens, 11, 26, 112-15
police, 1, 3-4, 6-8, 10, 18, 25, 27, 39, 43-4, 69, 93-5, 101, 104, 106-7, 110, 113, 115, 117, 119, 122, 126-30, 132, 140
poor relief, 37, 44
prostitutes, 26, 41, 44, 67, 72, 118, 122, 125-27
Protestant work ethic, 37

race, 17, 92
red-light district, 25, 115, 118, 123, 125-6, 129
Rendell, Ruth, 72-3, 146
rent-boys, 128
research tourist, 31
right to buy, 102
rogue pamphlets, 50-2, 65
Rough Sleepers' Initiative, 18, 41, 101, 132, 146

shadow work, 104, 120, 122, 130
Shakespeare, William, 74-5, 146
Shaw, George Bernard, 79, 146
Shelter, 40, 42, 141, 146
Shrewsbury, 3, 107, 109, 140
Shropshire, 3, 17, 104, 107, 109, 140
Skid row, 20-1, 113
space, 13, 18, 22-3, 25, 27, 31-2, 36, 76-9, 82-7, 97, 99, 102, 104, 106-7, 109-11, 113, 115, 118-19, 120, 122-3, 126-7, 129-30, 141, 146-7
Stoke-on-Trent, 18, 37, 90
Straw, Jack, 36, 101

150

151